Second Steps

A guide to setting up a business in the craft world

Cover image:
Contemporary Ceramics
Marshall Street, London

Compiled and edited by
Caroline Mornement

Published by BCF Books
Burton Cottage Farm, East Coker, Yeovil
Somerset BA22 9LS
2006

Printed by Creeds the Printers
Broadoak, Dorset

Distribution: BCF Books
On line sales: www.bcfbooks.co.uk.

T: 01935 862731
F: 01935 863333
E cm@craftgalleries.co.uk
ISBN-10 0-9550026-2-1
ISBN-13 978-0-9550026-2-5

Acknowledgments:

I would like to thank the following
who, although busy with their own craft businesses,
agreed to share their career experiences
with Second Steps.

Sandra Bosanquet, Julian Belmonte, Neil Bottle,
Alison Branagan, Matthew Burt,
Pamela Campanelli, Jane Charles, Willie Carter,
Rachael Chambers, Gina Frost, Rachel Gogerly,
Paul Grantham, Danielle Holmes,
Andy Green-Howard, Sara Harris, Kathleen Hills,
Gareth Huxtable, Clare John, Rosemary Jones,
John McKellar, Jo Mitchell, Chris Noble,
Dillon Rudge, Carrie Shapiro,
Jeff Soan and Robyn West.

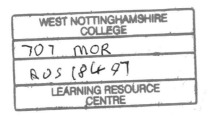

Although every effort has been made to ensure that the
information given in this book is correct at the time of
publication, the publishers cannot accept responsibility
for any errors.

Contents

Contents

Profile of the Editor

After studying at St Martins College of Art & Design and Hammersmith School of Art in the 1960's I pursued a successful career as an interior designer in London.

However, in 1984, after marriage and four children, I set up a craft gallery in converted stables in Somerset. In 1988 I opened a second gallery in Salisbury. Alongside the galleries, I continued 'making': designing and painting furniture, and carving decoy ducks.

During this time I also spent ten years helping to set up and run a community arts centre in Somerset. Here I liaised between artists to organise exhibitions, work-shops and educational residencies, and I waded through the constant preparation of applications for funding.

I was also on the steering committee for the first and subsequent Somerset Art Weeks, which provided me with opportunities to learn about the problems of country-based artists and makers.

In 1993 I closed both of my galleries in order to concentrate on editing the Craft Galleries Guides, which was first published the previous year.

Gaining a degree in Arts Administration in 1996 from Somerset College of Arts & Technology has helped with every aspect of my work.

I hope that some of the experiences I have gained in my varied and enjoyable career can be passed on to help others avoid some of the pitfalls that may be met – but avoided – in pursuit of an enjoyable and profitable craft career.

Introduction

There has been a dramatic change in our communication technology in the past eight years. The first Second Steps, published in 1998, included very few websites; now there is scarcely one contact without a web presence.

So do you still need Second Steps as a guide to get you started? Yes, although the aim of this concise book remains the same i.e. **to bring all the information you need together and direct your thoughts** and although you now have the internet, just a mouse away, opening doors to an endless source of information; **you still need to know what to look for** which involves serious research and planning.

This book leads you through the different areas to be considered at the various stages, giving plenty of contacts to pursue the topic further. Wherever possible sections are illustrated with case studies by makers, gallery owners and others who share their expertise and experience. These provide a useful source of advice and will help and encourage you on your journey to find the right way for you to get started on a career in the craft world.

Caroline Mornement

Selling Yourself

Kathleen Hills - Milkii

Selling Yourself

Whichever route you are planning to take in order to sell your work, you will need a smart Self Promotional kit with which to sell yourself. It is well worth taking time to prepare a professional package. As ✳ **you are the most important product** you will ever have to sell, get it right now and you are half way there.

Although many of you will already have a CV, I have been amazed to discover that some students have still been given no guidance on the best way to prepare one. So have patience with a rather basic start.

Whilst checking websites for this article I read that many employers are rejecting paper CVs in favour of electronic ones, according to a survey recruiters said that if they had to choose between two equal candidates, one with a paper CV and one with an electronic one, they would pick the electronic CV first every time.

Both practical and emotional reasons lie behind growing anti-paper prejudice. Recruiters say it is faster and more efficient to deal with electronic CVs, whether they arrive by e-mail, through a company's own web site, or from an external Internet job site. According to the writer of this website gem '*sending CVs via email isn't just a luxury anymore, it's a necessity!'*

✳ Time spent now, preparing your 'self promotion kit', will benefit you in the future.

CV

Regardless of which style you choose - post or email, you still have to consider the content of your CV very carefully and should try to be as concise as possible.

As you will have gathered your CV is a **very important tool**. This may be the first contact a prospective employer/venue host/funder has with you. It will show just how serious and professional you are, giving the reader confidence to deal with you and a desire to meet you to discuss the job/commission further. It needs to be :

- concise,

- well researched,

- targeted towards the job/grant etc., which may mean revising your text each time,

- regularly updated, with new shows/commissions,

- presented clearly and professionally, preferably on one side of A4.

The information given should include :

- your education, particularly further qualifications,

- exhibitions in which you have taken part both joint and solo,

CV

- Any awards which you have received,

- Residencies and workshops which you may have run,

- Commissions of importance.

- Work which you have carried out, even unpaid, if it is relevant to the particular job/grant etc.

- Anything, which will confirm that you have the necessary abilities to carry out a project from start to finish.

- Dredge through your past experiences to see what might be useful to help emphasise your skills.

- In some cases it may be relevant to include a career plan, which might also include the hope for further training opportunities.

Then go back through your list choosing the items which are ✴ **really** relevant and consider how to incorporate them into your CV.

✴ Be brutal with your editing, only keep what is really relevant to the application.

CV

When applying for a job, grant or award it is important to check back with the brief (criteria) to see that your CV covers the skills and information required, editing it if necessary, to remove irrelevant details.

Your CV is an advertisement to sell you, and usually you only have one chance to make an impression on the reader. Think of some descriptive and positive words to describe your abilities and include these, to help sell yourself. Many CV's are just a boring list of events with nothing to make them jump out at the reader.

Remember that your CV may be one of 50 or more which the reader has to wade through. Why should they bother with yours?

To keep the reader's attention:

- use short paragraphs, highlighting sections with an asterisk,

- Check your spelling and grammar,

- **Don't exaggerate your abilities,**

- Don't include a picture of yourself.

When needed enclose a clear but ✳ short covering letter, explaining your special reason for believing yourself to be suitable. Be positive but not over enthusiastic. Where relevant include a career plan as well as the usual list of experiences. Throughout try to keep your application concise and to the point. Use matching paper for CV, letter and envelope to present a professional image.

If you are applying for a job, rather than promoting yourself as a self employed maker, you may wish to consider an idea suggested in the Guardian. Rather than a traditional CV they advised using a single sheet of A4 to highlight four main areas.

Personal details as mentioned earlier

Personal Promise

Who you are, how you do it and what you do. All explained in a clear style, to create a 'sound bite' promoting the essence of you.

Core competence

To describe your characteristics, things you have achieved and the skills you needed to do them. Maybe running a campaign, debating, putting on an exhibition all these would have needed particular skills.

Career & Academic details

These would include the standard education details plus any work experience or exhibition details.

✳ Your letter is a chance to reveal more of your personality but don't get carried away.

CV

As mentioned earlier the Internet has become one of the most popular ways for employers to receive CV's but it is also the easiest way to send them. You can quickly contact anyone who needs to know about you or receive applications, proposals etc. it is even good for setting up online interviews with your future employer, gallery or client. Further advice for on-line applications suggestions included the following:

Cover Letters

"Please find my CV attached" isn't a convincing enough reason for the employer to consider you. You still need the cover letter which is your first sales pitch to a potential employer, as described earlier (page 12).

Your Email Address

Set up an email address just for job searching and work related projects. Have a normal e-mail name, ✳ **not** blondie@aol.com or hotstud@yahoo.com. You may very well be these things, but keep these email addresses for your personal use and appear business like.

> ✳ This is a good point, which I also heard made at a talk at the New Designers. The speaker reminded graduates that the time had come to move on from the sexy/funky image they may have wished to promote when at university – now it was time to get down to business.

CV/Photographs

Keep a Job/Commission etc Tracking Sheet

Create a file with every job/work application. This includes everything from printing out the job advertisement and your application to taking note of the day you applied etc. Keep notes of all phone calls and correspondence as well as your research.

For more advice about preparing CV's, many give examples try:
www.thegraduate.co.uk
www.careercraft.co.uk
www.nottingham.ac.uk/careers/apps&cvs
www.netjobs.co.uk
www.a-n.co.uk

General 'setting up a business' advice:
www.artquest.org.uk
www.artsadvice.com

Association of Photographers
81 Leonard Street
EC2A 4QS
T: 020 7739 6669
www.theaop.org
Provides an information service.

Photographs

A selection of top quality, strong, clear, well focused images, of your work is essential for your self promotion package - how else can the viewer judge if your work is interesting to them?

If your work is varied, try to include several images to give the broad picture of what you can do. However, make sure that the work sent is relevant to the application/proposal/exhibition etc. and that you will be able to supply something similar if required i.e not out of date work.

It is a good idea to get into the habit of keeping a photographic record of all your work, in case one of your best pieces sells quickly and you have no record of a particular masterpiece, with which to tempt others.

You should consider looking for a photographer who will be sympathetic to your work. If you have been impressed by a professionals' work and seen that they can take good pictures of work similar to yours it would be ✳ **well worth the investment** at this stage. You will then have a set of top quality photos with which to sell your work, or apply for funding etc.

✳ Throughout this edition of Second Steps writers are consistently saying that you **must** supply good images. Unless you really are an amazing photographer it is almost essential to invest in paying a professional to provide you with a good set of photos **now**.

Photographs

You might be able to share the cost with a group of friends by asking the photographer to hold a session, at one venue. In this way you may each acquire a set of good quality photos of your own work. You might also persuade a photographer to agree to barter his work for a piece of yours.

If you do use a professional photographer agree a price before giving the go ahead and clarify the copyright situation. The copyright is his unless he has given you a written agreement passing it on to you. You will probably want to reproduce a photo or two at some stage, so you must be clear that he has given written permission for them to be used. You should always credit his name alongside the photo.

Alternatively, if you are still at university, (or still have contacts) perhaps you can take advice from technical staff, persuade them to take some photographs for you or even learn to use the dark room. In this way you may be able to prepare your own set of photos before leaving and being launched into the real world.

If you are taking your own photographs, the following appear to be the main points made by expert advisers:

- Consider the strong points of your work and make sure that your images will emphasise these i.e is your work about colour, shape, originality, strong design etc.

Photographs

- Be clear what the image is for, is it to sell a particular piece to the public, to sell your body of work to an exhibition venue, to a gallery or for selection for a trade show ✳?

- Is it for a grant application? e.g if it is for an award it will need to be eye catching, as it will be one of a large number being viewed.

- Use a film with a low I.S.A. rating which will result in sharper more detailed images.

- Where possible use a tripod or equivalent stand to steady the camera.

- If using sunlight try to avoid shafts of light on the subject but aim for a broad even spread of light.

- Try to position the camera as close and as square on as possible to the object.

- Prepare a simple neutral back ground.

- Consider very carefully before including a model, this can be a distraction and is not often a success.

✳ If you need your images returned **do** remember to enclose the correct size SAE + correct value of stamps.

Photographs

Check out the possibility of attending a local photographic workshop. Guilds and Regional Art Council of England offices sometimes run short courses.

There are many more useful tips on how to display your work, with suitable backgrounds, spotlight reflectors, light filters etc. **in a six page technical leaflet** available from ❋ The Crafts Council of Ireland.

Sending images with your applications:
When choosing which photos to use for a particular application, take advice from a friend as it can be very difficult to look at your own work dispassionately.

Labelling
Whatever photographs/slides are used remember to either label each image clearly with your name, address/tel no, medium, size, (if this would be helpful), a title where needed and an arrow to indicate the top for viewing (unless really obvious). Sticky labels on slides may catch in the projector so it is better to use a permanent marker pen. Alternatively you could include a typed list of the images sent, numbered if there are several, giving each a short description - as before remember to include your name and contact details, and always credit the photographer where necessary.

❋ Contact to request leaflet:
The Crafts Council of Ireland, Castle Yard
T: 00353 5677 61804   E: caroline@ccoi.ie

Photographs

Packing

If you are sending a print be sure to pack it carefully with a card/rigid plastic support and a label stuck on the back of the print with all the details

Slides are now hardly used but if you are sending any they are best presented in plastic holders or multi sheets and it is advisable **not to use glass slides** which nearly always break in transit. Do not use too much packing and tape which can be **very** frustrating and time consuming for the person who receives them.

Digital images:

The majority of images are now supplied digitally as JPEG's or TIFF's. If they are required for re-printing purposes they must be saved at a minimum of 300dpi and usually printers like them saved in CMYK.

I cannot emphasise enough how important it is to check that the image you send is saved at 300dpi (not changed after it has been taken via Photoshop).

Reduce size to email:

If you plan to send an image via email, reduce it to a zipped file if possible, as you do not want to clog up the receivers email and annoy them.

Label carefully:

Also take time to label your digital file clearly, write your name and a short relevant tag e.g. J.Smith raku vase. Do not call them ❊ POT 1, 2 etc. with no name or just leave the film reference numbers which will make no sense at all.

Photographs

CD's

Do not send a CD full of all your work with a message saying 'see no 56349', why should the viewer sort through to find the one in question? They won't.

It is best to sort your images and select those required for that particular application, then burn the CD making sure that each image was clearly labelled first. Many makers now design their own CD covers with name and contact details plus a print of one or two small images; this presents your work in a professional manner.

Hard Copy

If you are supplying a digital image for re-printing do send a hard copy with the colour as true as possible. As editor of the Craft Galleries Guide I can assure you it is very hard to be working in the dark, so to speak, not knowing what the image should look like. If you send a computer print-out as your hard copy do use glossy paper so that the image will be sharper

Alternative

An alternative to a photo is to scan a flat piece of work. This can provide a record of work but check carefully to see if the finish is good enough to use for promotional purposes.

※ You might be amazed how many JPEG's are emailed, when researching for the Craft Galleries Guide, just labelled 'Gallery interior or exterior'. Try to make life easy for the person you are dealing with.

Photography by Paul Grantham

Marketing your work with flexible photography

As you generate a body of work and start to market both your product and yourself, you will often become involved with the production of product photographs.

What makes an effective marketing image?

You will be presenting to a professional audience. Avoiding pitfalls such as photography with less than complimentary backgrounds like carpets is a must, as this reflects badly on both you and your work. If you decide to produce your own photography then take as much care and planning with producing the images as you do with your work.

Good practice is to plan well and ask: What do you want to use them for? Who else will use them? How do you get published coverage and a positive feedback?

Wow factor images like close ups, small details and creative lighting are fantastic for getting attention and forcing people to look and want to see more.This will be an emotional feedback based on the actual photograph and not necessarily on the work. Wow shots will get published, but with reduced success rate if you are trying to get your images into articles as more work is required at the publishers end.

Practical images are the most important element of a flexible photographic collection. All clients want to know is what the actual work looks like; the best way to achieve this is using a clean white background with the entire product in plain view.

Photography by Paul Grantham

White backgrounds make objects easy to cut out and use in endless graphic design possibilities (see below). Galleries will be able to make a true judgement on your work and will be more likely to trust that what they see is what they will get. Flexibility is the key to good marketing photographs, if you plan well you can use a limited number of shots to produce all of your material.

23

Post Cards

Many artists and makers use postcards as a multi-purpose tool. Once you have an image that you are really pleased with, it may be worth the extra expense of ordering cards from one of the many card printers.

For a reasonable fee you can ❋ order 1000 cards and include up to 50 words, on the reverse, to advertise yourself giving your address and any other useful information. The card can then be used in many situations:

- as invitations to exhibitions,

- reminders for potential clients to take away from shows/workshop/exhibitions,

- to introduce yourself to galleries,

- in place of business cards etc.

Research through relevant art magazines will soon give you a selection of addresses to contact. Once you have found a company offering what you need, at the right price, it is once again essential to provide a really clear image.

❋ Several card suppliers advertise regularly in the back of the Crafts Magazine or just check **www.yell.com** or **google** for post card suppliers and make your own comparisons.

Press Cuttings/Websites

Press cuttings are another useful form of self promotion. From the start of your career try to keep any editorials, reviews and Private View invitations which may have images of your work included etc. If they are to be shown to a prospective employer/gallery owner be sure to present them as neatly as possible, and remember to clearly date them.

Whenever making a presentation or application present all your work, portfolio, photos, forms, (whatever is involved) etc. in a professional manner. Check that none of the packaging material looks tatty or worn, make sure everything is labelled clearly and can be read in a logical manner with all images facing the right way. Keep a list of all that you include, then if you are persuaded to leave your portfolio, you will know exactly what should be returned to you. Always ask for a receipt and check that you have covered the copyright issues (see 126).

Websites

As the majority of makers have their own websites before they leave university or soon afterwards the need for press cutting folders is fading. Instead makers will want to keep a list of all their publicity on their website, alongside a list of their exhibitions and career history. I have been very impressed with some that I have seen recently and recommend Kathleen Hill's **www.multi.co.uk** as an excellent example.

See Internet section for more ideas p233

A Note from the Arts Council of England

Arts Council England is the national arts development agency, funded from both National Lottery and Treasury grant–in–aid. We provide leadership for the crafts in England with our partners including the Crafts Council. We aim to strengthen the craft economy and infrastructure of specialist crafts centres and workspaces. Grants for individual makers are available from our Grants for the Arts programme through our regional offices. We fund work which demonstrates :

- innovation in aesthetic vision,

- an understanding of the quality of materials used,

- an investigation of process and the exercise of artistic control over the production process, including batch production,

- personal enquiry and development of individual practice,

- understanding of the diverse cultural context of craft practice,

- the highest standard of skills and making.

We encourage culturally diverse makers and the participation of disabled people in the crafts sector. We do not prioritise traditional or heritage craft that reproduces or restores.

Our new publication Making it to Market, launched at the Crafts Council's Collect fair in February 2006, shows the potential for growth. Our Own Art scheme is helping with interest loans up to £2000 for the purchase of contemporary art and craft through venues countrywide. We are also working with museums to commission new work and to develop public collections of contemporary craft.

Arts Councils

Arts Council of England
Head Office
14 Great Peter Street
SW1P 2NQ
T: 0845 300 6200
E: enquiries@artscouncil.org.uk
www.artscouncil.org.uk

N.B. Contact details for **all** Arts Council of England Offices

The Crafts Council
44a, Pentonville Road
N1 9BY
T: 020 7278 7700
E: reference@craftscouncil.org.uk
www.craftscouncil.org.uk

Crafts Council of Ireland
Castle Yard,
Kilkenny
T: 00353 56776 1804
E: info@ccoi.ie
www.craftscouncil-of-ireland.ie

Northern Ireland Arts Council
MacNeice House
77 Malone Road
Belfast BT9 6AQ
T: 028 9038 5200
E: info@artscouncil-ni.org
www.artscouncil-ni.org

Arts Councils

Scottish Arts Council
12 Manor Place
Edinburgh EH3 7DD
T: 0845 603 6000
E: help.desk@scottisharts.org.uk
www.scottisharts.org.uk

Mid & West Wales
6 Gardd Llydaw
Jackson Lane
Carmarthen SQA31 1QD
T: 01267 234248

ACWales Central & SWales Offices
9 Museum Place
Cardiff
CF10 3NX
Central T: 029 2037 6500
South Wales T: 029 2037 6525
E: feedback@artswales.org.uk
www.acw.org.uk

North Wales
36 Prince's Drive
Colwyn Bay
LL29 8LA
T: 01492

Arts Councils of England

Arts Council of England
These contact details will lead you to all the
Arts Council of England offices:
T: 0845 300 6200
E: enquiries@artscouncil.org.uk
www.artscouncil.org.uk

Arts Council England, East
Eden House
48-49 Bateman Street
Cambridge
CB2 1LR
Arts Council England, East Midlands
St Nicholas Court
25-27 Castle Gate
Nottingham
NG1 7AR

Arts Council England, London
2 Pear Tree Court
EC1R 0DS

Arts Council England, North East
Central Square
Forth Street
Newcastle upon Tyne
NE1 3PJ

Arts Councils of England

Arts Council England, North West
Manchester House
22 Bridge Street
Manchester
M3 3AB

Arts Council of England, South East
Sovereign House
Church Street
Brighton
BN1 1RA

Arts Council England South West
Senate Court
Southernhay
Exeter
EX1 1UG

Arts Council England West Midlands
82 Granville Street
Birmingham, B1 2LH

**Arts Council England
Yorkshire Arts**
21 Bond Street
Dewsbury
WF13 1AX

Databases

Ladies in Jaisalmer - networking

Guilds

Another useful way to promote yourself, with minimal expense, is to apply for membership of your regional relevant Craft Guild/Association.

Each will vary in its requirements for applications and membership fees. Once you are a member of a guild you will benefit from:

- the opportunity to exhibit work in their exhibitions,

- opportunity to attend lectures and seminars,

- the support of other like minded people (some with experience to share),

- the kudos of being able to add membership status to your CV.

Art Workers Guild
Secretary - Monica Grose-Hodge
6 Queen Square
WC1 N3AT
T: 020 7713 0966
E: monica@artworkersguild.org
www.artworkersguild.org
Established in 1824, membership by nomination.
Fees £85 per year for those living within M25 area and £50 for those outside.

Guilds

The Devon Guild of Craftsmen
Riverside Mill
Bovey Tracey
TQ13 9AF
T: 01626 832223
E: devonguild@crafts.org.uk
www.crafts.org.uk
Membership by invitation following selection meetings,
restricted to those living/working in the South West of
England, publishes a newsletter. Fee £85

Embroiderers' Guild
Apartment 41
Hampton Court Palace
Surrey
KT8 9AU
T: 020 8943 1229
E: administrator@embroiderersguild.org.uk
www.embroiderersguild.org.uk

East Sussex Guild of Craftworkers
Membership Secretary Mrs. M. Althorpe
27 Boughton Lane
Maidstone
Kent
ME15 9QN
T: 01622 744464

Guilds

Guild of Glass Engravers
The Secretary
87 Nether Street
N12 7NP
T: 020 8446 4050
www.gge/.org.uk
Aims to provide and promote the highest qualities of design in glass.

Gloucestershire Guild of Craftsman
Jan Bunyan/Mary Noble
Guild Gallery, Painswick Centre
Bisley St, Painswick
GL6 6QQ
T: 01452 814746
E: info@guildcrafts.org.uk
www.guildcrafts.org.uk

Guild of Herefordshire Craftsmen
Alison Payne
Bartons Well
Much Marcle
Nr Ledbury
HR8 2LY
www.herefordcraftguild.org.uk
They offer three honourary places to students each year provided they are Hereford based, including sponsorship for one year.

Guilds

Guild of Master Craftsmen
Castle Place
166 High Street
Lewes
BN7 1XU
T: 01273 488005
www.thegmsgroup.com
Membership covers a wide range of those who earn a living from their crafts or trades. Publishes a variety of magazines including the Knitting Magazine which can all be bought on line.

Oxfordshire Craft Guild
Membership Secretary
7 Goddards Lane
Chipping Norton
OX7 5NP
E: info@oxfordshirecraftguild.co.uk
www.oxfordshirecraftguild.co.uk

The Art & Craft Guild of Lancashire
83 Elmers Green
Skelmersdale
WN8 6SG
T: 01695 733428
E: info@artandcraftguild.co.uk
www.artandcraftguild.co.uk

Guilds

Norfolk Craftsmen's Guild
Chairman Peter Kingsland
Rosecroft, Rode Lane
Carleton Rode
Norwich
NR16 1NW
T: 01953 860706
Membership restricted to those living in East Anglia
Joining fee £5, annual £25.

Northamptonshire Guild of Designer Craftsmen
Secretary Bob Walder
28 High Street
Northampton,
NN7 3AS
T: 01604 858470 p.m.
E: bobwalder@compuserve.com

Somerset Guild of Craftsmen
Peter Cottell
Laurel Cottage
Isle Abbotts
Taunton
TA3 6HN
T: 01460 281550
E: sgcsec@supanet.com
www.somersetguild.co.uk

Guilds

Sussex Guild
Guild Secretary Judith Cooper
The Gate House
Flowers Green
Herstmonceux
BN27 1RL
T: 01323 833239
E: info@thesussexguild.co.uk
www.thesussexguild.co.uk
A network of professional designer/makers from Sussex
and adjoining counties, whose work is selected for both
skill and innovation. The Guild mounts six to eight Craft
Shows every year in a variety of venues. For
membership application form or a current programme
contact the Guild Secretary.

Chartered Society of Designers
5 Bermondsey Exchange
179-181 Bermondsey St
SE1 3UW
T: 020 7357 8088
E: csd@csd.org.uk
www.csd.org.uk
Membership (granting status of Chartered Designer) is
open to all graduates of exhibition, graphic, interior,
product,textile or fashion design. Support is offered to
help smooth the transition from studying to work.
Members are on hand to provide advice and run.

Societies

surgeries. There are events and training, reduced insurance and legal advice. A bi-monthly magazine and regular meetings. Joining fee £45 per year (for graduates). Each year all second year design students on any full-time design course around the world are invited to submit a piece of work for scrutiny by a panel of CSD and design industry judges.

The Society of Bookbinders
E: info@societyofbookbinders.com
Also has eight regional contacts
www.societyofbookbinders.com
Now has eight regional branches see website for contact details. Full membership £32 or £22 for those aged 25. years and under.

Contemporary Glass Society
c/o Broadfield House Glass Museum
Compton Drive
Kingswinford
West Midlands
DY6 9NS
T: 01603 507737
E: admin@cgs.org.uk
www.cgs.org.uk
The Contemporary Glass Society (CGS) is a non-profit making limited company by guarantee founded with dual objectives of encouraging excellence in glass as a

Societies

creative medium and developing a greater awareness and appreciation of contemporary glass world wide. Membership is open to anyone interested in contemporary glass.
Membership £20 for students £30 for individuals.

Norfolk Contemporary Craft Society
Jennifer Boland, Secretary
The White House
Town Street
Hickling
NR12 0AY
T: 01692 598747
E: secretary@norfolkcraft.co.uk
www.norfolkcraft.co.uk

Royal Birmingham Society of Artists
4 Brook Street
St. Paul's
Birmingham B3 1SA
T: 0121 236 4353
E: secretary@rbsa.org.uk
www.rbsa.org.uk
Join as a 'Friend' for £18.00 which enables free entry into open exhibitions plus invites to all private views and a newsletter.

Societies

The Society of Designer Craftsmen
The Secretary
24 Rivington Street
EC2A 3DU
T: 020 7739 3663
E: info@societyofdesigncraftsmen.org.uk
www.societyofdesigncraftsmen.org.uk
The Society of Designer Craftsmen is the largest and oldest multi-craft society in Britain. The work of members ranges across all the craft disciplines. The aim of the Society is to emphasise designer-making where innovation, originality and quality are paramount.

Selective membership is open to people with a strong and innovative design sense, who also have the crafts-manship and sensitivity to materials used to make the objects they design. See web for forms etc.

Suffolk Craft Society
Secretary - Monique Gregson
Brisge Green Farm
Gissing Road
Burston
Norfolk
E: organiser@suffolkcraftsociety.org
www.suffolkcraftsociety.org

Societies

Textile Society
Secretary-June Morris
17 Geneva Avenue
Malvern
WR14 3PX
www.textilesociety.org.uk
Send SAE for details
Aims to unite all those interested in the study of textiles.

Bristol Potters
www.ukpotters.co.uk

British Woodcarvers Association
Membership Secretary
4 William Road
Cuxton
Kent
ME2 4DL
www.bwa-woodcarving.fsnet.co.uk
Regional groups seek to increase aesthetic awareness between members and public through exhibitions and demonstrations, locally and nationally. Publishes a quarterly newsletter 'Woodcarvers' Gazette'.

Associations

Cornwall Crafts Association
Trelowarren Craft Gallery
Mawgan
Nr Helston
TR12 6AF
T: 01326 221567
www.cornwallcrafts.co.uk

Dorset Arts & Crafts Association
Paul Mewsome
21 St. Anthony's Road
Bournemouth
BH2 6PB
T: 01202 553113
E:info@dorsetartsandcrafts.org
www.dorsetartsandcrafts.org

Craft Potters Association
7 Marshall Street
W1F 7EH
T: 020 7437 7605
E: cpa@ceramics.com
www.cpaceramics.com
Originally formed as a co-operative for potters in 1958.
The CPA is now open to everyone working with
ceramics. It offers exhibitions and a sales area and
organises lectures, visits and demonstrations
The CPA also publishes a bi-monthly magazine 'Ceramic

Associations

Review' and produces 'Potters' an illustrated book which lists all the Members of the Association, currently in its 11th edition. CPA News is a bi-monthly newsletter of some dozen pages which is distributed to all Members. It includes a variety of articles, notices, reviews, members' letters and advertisements.
Members' work is displayed at the Marshall Street Gallery - see front cover.

The Craft Pottery Charitable Trust was established in 1991 and each year awards bursaries to enable students to carry out individual projects. (see Grants p289)
There is an annual 'Setting Up' exhibition for new potters, names must be submitted by colleges, two from each will be selected.

Membership

There are three categories of membership: associate, professional and Fellow. Anyone with an interest in ceramics may apply for Associate membership, but the Professional & Fellows are selected by the CPA Council

Students

Membership fees are substantially reduced for students. Attendance at workshops, lectures and demonstrations organised by the Association is also subsidised for students. A member of Council has responsibility for liaison with students and their college.

Associations

East Anglian Potters Association
Membership Secretary
Tony Pugh
Vine Leigh Cottage
Main Street
Wardy Hill
Ely, CB6 2DF
T: 01353 778462
E: tonypugh@onetel
www.the-eapa.org

The Association for Contemporary Jewellery
PO Box 37807
London
SE23 1XJ
T: 020 8291 4201
E: enquiries@acj.org.uk
www.acj.org.uk
Publishes a useful newsletter/magazine 'Findings'.

Kent Potters Association
www.kentpotters.co.uk

London Potters Association
www.londonpotters.com
A voluntary charitable organisation and one of the
largest pottery associations in the UK. Membership is
open to anyone with an interest in ceramics.

Associations

Midland Potters Association
Membership Secretary - Helen Wills
44 Hollyhurst Road
Sutton Coldfield
B73 6DSY
T: 0121 605 4947
E: emailmpa@yahoo.co.uk
www.midlandspotters.pwp.blueyonder.co.uk
Membership covers 73 all Midlands based
people interested in clay. Exhibitions, events, monthly
MPA News and a slide index.

The National Association of Disabled Craftworkers
Piethorn Cottage
Barrachan By Mochrum
Newton Stewart
DG8 9NF
T: 01988 860 204
Aims to help disabled makers, their families/helpers gain
the information needed to carry out their chosen craft.

North West Disability Arts Forum
MPAC Building
1-27 Bridport Street
LIverpool L3 5QF
T: 0151 707 1733
E: info@nwdaf.co.uk
www.nwdaf.co.uk

Associations

Northern Potters Association
Membership Secretary Catherine Boyne-Whitelegg
E: willardwhitelegg@aol.co
www.northern-potters.org.uk
Membership open to potters and others interested in clay. Organises exhibitions seminars and events, discounted subs to AN.

Rural Crafts Association
Heights Cottage
Brook Road
Wormley
Surrey
GU8 5UA
www.ruralcraftsassociation.co.uk

Scottish Potters Association
E: info@scottishpotters.org
www.scottishpotters.co.uk
Membership open to all potters. Organises events, demonstrations and exhibitions.

Westcountry Potters Association
www.westcountrypotters.co.uk
Open to anyone interested in pottery in Devon, Cornwall, Somerset, Dorset.
Membership fee £25.

Associations/Groups

The Assoc. of British Woodturners
Roger Pugh
76 Towers Road
Poynton
Cheshire
SK12 1DF
T: 01625 874818
www.britishwoodturners.co.uk

Applied Arts Scotland
Edinburgh College of Arts
School of Design and Applied Arts
Hunter Building
Lauriston Place
EH3 9DF
T: 0131 221 6143
E: office@appliedartsscotland.org.uk
www.craftscotland.org
Supports applied arts in Scotland, join for £25 per year.

The Art House
The Art House
Wakefield College
Margaret Street,
Wakefield WF1 2DH
T: 01924 377 740
E: info@theart.house
www.the-arthouse.org.uk

Groups

Crafts Council National Register of Makers
www.craftscouncil.org.uk/ref
A comprehensive listing of craftspeople and a valuable
resource for shops, galleries, buyers and businesses

Contemporary Applied Arts
2 Percy Street
London
W1T 1DD
T: 020 7436 2344
E: info@caa.org.uk
www.caa.org.uk
Founded in 1948 this was the original Craft Centre for
Great Britain. Now represents 300 makers who exhibit
and sell their work through the Percy Street Gallery.
Professionals working in the applied arts in the British
Isles may apply for membership.

Designer Bookbinders
The Secretary
6 Queen Square
WC1N 3AR
E: secretary@designerbookbinders.org.uk
www.designerbookbinders.org.uk
Non-selective membership open to anyone interested in
bookbinding and in the art of the book.

Groups

The British Furniture Makers
www.bfm.org.uk/
The Furniture Makers Company
Furniture Makers' Hall
12 Austin Friars
EC2N 2HE
T: 020 7256 5558
E:clerk@furnituremkrs.cop.uk
www.furnituremkrs.co.uk
A charity whose aims are to promote the design, manufacture and retail of British furniture. To offer awards, bursaries and prizes. Arrange conferences that will promote craftsmanship and training and to provide for needy members of the Trade, The Company and their dependents.

North Wales Potters
Membership Secretary
Susan Morgan
Myrddin
Ala Uchaf
Pwllheli
LL53 5RE
www.northwalespotters.co.uk
Membership open to professional potters and those interested in ceramics who live in North Wales & Deeside region.

Groups

South West Textile Group
Sara Maddocks
T: 01364 72997
E: semaddocks@yahoo.com
www.southwesttextilegroup.org.uk

South Wales Potters
www.southwalespotters.org.uk

designGAP
607 B The Big Peg
120 Vyse Street
Hockley
Birmingham
B16 6NF
T: 0121 242 0242
E: designgap04@yahoo.co.uk
www.design-gap.co.uk
Designer makers have a website under umbrella of
Design Gap- a charity keen to promote the work of
new and established artists, they also publish a
trade catalogue.

Publications

There are many craft related magazines and publications which are useful to keep up to date with what is going on in your particular medium and for inspiration and reference. Some of the best are:

a-n The Artists Information Company
7-15 Pink Lane
Newcastle upon Tyne
NE1 5DW,
T: +44 (0)191 241 8000
E: info@a-n.co.uk
www.a-n.co.uk
a-n is a vital resource for artists at all career stages and all who engage and collaborate with them. As well as publishing a-n Magazine, a-n provides material around issues like negotiating contracts and professional practice, as well as access to hundreds of jobs and opportunities including commissions, residencies and competitions.
The Artists' Fees and Payments series includes Establishing a charge rate for a working artist; Good practice in paying artists and Good exhibition practice, in print and online.A subscription costs from £28 for artists, or take a one month trial for £5.

Publications

A-N Artists Newsletter (General/practical advice)
See previous page for details

Ceramic Review (Ceramics) also see advert p311
T: 0207 439 3377
E: info@ceramicreview.com

Craft Galleries Guide (Resource to find outlets)
T: 01935 862731
E: cm@craftgalleries.co.uk
www.bcfbooks.co.uk

Crafts Magazine (Crafts)
T: 020 77806 2538
E:crafts@craftscouncil.org.uk

also Makers News
T: 020 7278 7700
E: makersnews@craftscouncil.org.uk
www.craftscouncil.org.uk
www.ceramicreview.com

The Craftsman Magazine (Mixed crafts)
T: 01377 255213 also see advert p312
E: sales@craftsman-magazine.com
www.craftsman-magazine.com

Selvedge (Textiles)
T: 020 8341 9721
www.selvedge.org

Publications

Second Steps Portfolio
Entry in the portfolio is a good way to promote yourself to a wide range of buyers. The Portfolio, also published by BCF Books is produced annually and given free to nearly 300 galleries throughout the UK.

Entry in the booklet also gives makers the opportunity to have a web page designed and linked to: www.bcfbooks.co.uk

Previous participants are already reaping benefits as a number now appear in the 8th Craft Galleries Guide (a biannual BCF Book), having been invited by galleries who saw them first in the Portfolios.

Entry currently costs £50 + VAT for a page -
Application forms by post or download.
BCF Books, Burton Cottage Farm, East Coker, Yeovil
BA22 9LS **T:** 01935 862731
E: cm@craftgalleries.co.uk   **www.**bcfbooks.co.uk

Marketing

Market in Mysore - Southern India

Marketing

Chris Noble (tutor who wrote the Pricing section) says that he introduces marketing to his first year students, as he feels it is such an important part of the whole package. He encourages them to examine the market and rival products and to visualise their future place in their chosen market. In other words every decision becomes, to some extent, a marketing decision.✲ **Therefore any move which does not fit into this marketing plan should be questioned.**

Your market research and marketing plan should be included in your business plan. They will help explain, to your prospective funder, who your buyers will be and how you believe you will actually reach your sales targets.

Principal of Market Research should be to answer the following questions.

- What is your actual business to be and what do you hope to achieve?

- Who will your services/products appeal to?

- Is there a future market?

✲ Every decision connected to your business relates to the marketing plan.

Marketing

- How does your product or service meet the customer's needs?

- Who are your competitors? (if they do exist it means there is a market but you will have to work harder to share it).

- Calculate your price range and consider what sales you need to achieve a viable business.

Market Research for Product USP ✳

Does your product have a USP, Unique Selling Point. The idea being that a product should have a USP to make it different from the competition and to persuade people to buy it. It is worth taking time to consider your products and think how you could make them different in order to achieve a USP.

Just finding a niche market may not be sufficient, if the niche is too small and specialised there may not be sufficient buyers to give you a good income. Nor is it sufficient to compete on price alone, others can cut prices too.

Competition comes from all other traders, not just those selling similar products to yours. It is therefore

✳ It is hard to find a USP for some crafts, so maybe you have to work even harder at the standard of presentation, to make your work distinctive.

Marketing

necessary to look at the whole trading picture in your area. There is only so much money to go around and you have to think how your product will attract sufficient buyers to come in your direction.

Actual Market Research

The purpose is to test your product in the real world, so far the chances are that you have had success at college and selling or giving your work to friends and family. The hard truth will be revealed when you test your product in front of an unbiased market.

A graduation exhibition is a good opportunity, listen to the reactions of the public and read what they have to say in your comments book.※ Take the criticism as well as the praise and think about what is said. Also be observant about what others are doing, how they present their work and deal with interest and find sales outlets. You can quietly learn a lot from other people's mistakes and successes.

Talk to family and friends who already run businesses or work in a business. Visit as many relevant sales outlets as possible to see prices and presentation of comparative work. Read trade magazines and articles etc. to absorb as much about your subject as possible.

※ It is important to actually take note of the comments made and react accordingly, even if they are not complimentary.

Marketing

Try to decide which will be the best route for you to sell through to start off with. Will it be through **galleries, trade shows, retail shows, exhibitions, commissions, a manufacturer or a combination**? When you feel the time is right and your product is ready for public viewing approach a few suitable galleries and /or manufacturers and see what reaction and advice you get.

Competitors

Consider your competitors, how are they achieving their results, what are they offering that you are not, who are their customers? If they are well established try to discover how long it took them to reach the current point. (This may help you plan your cash flow see p93)

The customers - who will they be?

At this point in your market research you need to identify who your actual customers really will be, try to get a profile of one in your mind. You should clearly identify who you are trying to attract. If you are still not sure consider carefully the type of people who are likely to want to use your product. Perhaps a short questionnaire will help identify who your buyers are so you don't waste time targeting those who are unlikely to buy.

Marketing

Ask yourself:
  Will they be country loving ?
  Health fanatics, athletes, city workers ?

Where ?

  Having identified your public you need to consider :
Where they may live, what they may read i.e. local
papers, glossy magazines etc.
Other places they may visit - museums, local tourist
centre, sports centres etc.
Which restaurants/coffee shops they might frequent.
You need to build a really clear profile of who you are
targeting in order to aim your publicity directly at them.
Will you find them, locally or nationally?
At trade or retail outlets.

How ?

  Decide what methods you will use to alert them to
your product. You then need to consider how you can
do this within your budget and with the time you have
available. Will it be best to take out one expensive
advertisement in a glossy magazine and hope for the
best, or would it be better to run a series of cheaper
adverts in a local paper?
  Maybe advance entry in a Council Tourist brochure
might reach a wider audience. Alternatively you might
wish to produce a colour leaflet and plan strategic places
to leave them.

Marketing

Also talk to your potential buyers, find out what they think about your product and listen to their comments. ✳ It is easy to ask questions but ignore the answers because you don't want to make changes - these could be vital changes that influence future sales.

If you already have a web site make sure that you have the address on all your literature and every advertisement, so that readers can find out more about your product in their own time.

How much are your buyers likely to spend and will this be regularly, once a year or how often?

If they are buyers for a large shop this may well be a bulk order once a year, whereas a gallery owner might want small regular orders fulfiled. If you decide to sell through shows you will need to spread them through the year (if possible) so that you can keep your stocks level and avoid an enormous rush to produce work just for Christmas shows, for instance. Consider how you will fulfil all the orders - be realistic. This will help you decide if there is a future market and if not how could you create one? You will need to think hard about your product and if it is really what the customer wants, if not how could you improve on your design? **Try to put yourself into your customers shoes and think what makes them buy, when and where etc.**

✳ Listen and respond and be realistic with your plans.

Marketing

Planning your Marketing strategy

We must assume that you are happy with your product by this time, and believe that you have identified a unique aspect which will make your work stand out from that of your competitors. You will then need to create a plan, within your budget, to keep your regular customers and to bring in new business. Consider the best ways to do this and how much time it will take you to implement each month.

Advertising options:

- Posters regularly displayed in TIC's (tourists are usually in the mood to spend money).

- Adverts on the arts page of your local newspaper or free editorials (if you're lucky). ✳

- Glossy advert in national craft magazine
- A publicity leaflet, well distributed to hotels, B & B 's, other local tourist attractions, libraries, art centres etc.

- Flyers inserted in a magazine,

- An entry in a year book or relevant directory.

✳ Consider which publications to approach (not just locals) - some have art/lifestyle features - think ahead so that you catch them before their deadlines.

Marketing

Once you have decided on your advertising campaign, which could be a mix of the above or some other ideas, you will have to give careful thought to the best time to launch it. Will it be missed if it is near a major holiday? Should it be linked with another similar event which is happening in your locality? Is it better to wait until the weather is warmer? If you are going to send out direct mail, be selective so that there is not too much wastage - you can only expect an 8-10% return.

If making contact with clients by telephone or letter research before hand to get the right name, then be sure to target them. ☀ If you plan to take work to show new clients do not cold call, set up an appointment in advance, send written confirmation of the agreed date and time; this is an occasion when E-mail may be useful, otherwise letters are best.

Throughout your research keep a record of names and addresses to start your database, both for clients and media/press/trade contacts.

Style

The type of advertising you choose will depend on your budget. Regardless of your budget it is important to decide on a 'house style' and keep to this for all

☀ See Galleries section on how to approach new galleries as the same rules apply (p181).

Marketing

your publicity material. It can be as simple as always using the same colour paper, a small logo or the same font throughout. ✳

Your public will start to recognise any material that is yours and look out for it. Postcards can be used for private view invitations, just as reminders of your name and address with a strong image on the front or to write individual notes to patrons. Nearly all graduates now leave college with sophisticated business cards, with small images of their work included. These may have been supplied by your college as part of a bulk order for the end of year show. Another popular form of advertising is to present prospective buyers with a CD of their work, if you do try to design a cover card or at least supply thumbnail hard copy prints, to give some visual record of your work.

Press Release/Editorial

When writing your own publicity, particularly in the hope that an editor will notice it, how will your copy jump out of the pile and claim his/her attention? One way is to have an unusual angle in your text e.g. perhaps you make your pots while wearing a swimming costume, or work in a picturesque tree house. Anything,

✳ Design your 'house style/colour' before you start this campaign and then keep it for everything that is published/printed to promote your work.

Marketing

within reason, which the editor thinks will make a good picture. Obviously you should consider the particular publications point of view and try to angle your text to comply with this. Having been included in the paper your copy must also appeal to the readers and provide all the information which they need.

Essential information to include:

- Title of the event, with names of exhibitors

- Date, opening time and address

- Admission charges if relevant

- List of press photographs

- Press viewing date
- List any other reference material available

- Contact name, telephone number and email

Be enthusiastic, explain the benefit of your product over and above your rivals, pointing out your USP. Even though you are making pots, for instance, emphasise how they are different and need to be seen.

The Writers and Artists Year Book (available in most libraries) is a useful guide to press and media contacts Much more on Press Releases in next section.

Marketing

When preparing posters or leaflets the challenge is slightly different. The reader may check the top and bottom of the sheet and skim the central text block, so be sure to include the essentials in these areas. Try and choose a dynamic picture, line drawing or splash of colour to make your poster jump out at the reader as it is likely to be displayed on a board with many others alongside, distracting the viewer's attention.

If you have access to a computer it is useful to prepare a database of address labels for your press contacts. These could include local paper, national magazines and perhaps national papers, with their deadlines. This will save you hunting them out each time you wish to send out a press release.

It is helpful to send an image with your Press Release, as you will probably have emailed this just attach a JPEG. **Do** remember to make sure it is the right size-300dpi and clearly labelled. **Do not** send a selection which will clutter up the editor's desktop and take time to look through.

Even if you do not send a photograph have a selection of printed images/postcards ready at the event, in case a journalist visits and requests one. It is also advisable to have a copies of your press release ready to give as handouts to anyone interested.

Large organisations sometimes consider 'Marketing' as a philosophy. In marketing jargon this means focussing the customer from all areas of management,

Evaluation of Marketing

✳ **identifying, anticipating and satisfying the customer's requirements, profitably and efficiently.**

A small business should place the same importance on marketing and try to give sufficient time to develop a strategy. As I run my small publishing business as a sole trader, I know how difficult this is. If you are doing most jobs yourself, unlike the big firms who can employ someone to head each department, you have to manage your time very carefully and decide on your priorities.

Planning your marketing is not a one off chore, it will need to be monitored regularly to see if your first efforts were successful. You therefore need some targets to aim at. Marketing will be just one of many areas to be planned including the day to day planning.

Evaluation

When you have had some time to test the response of your advertising you will need to evaluate your success. Maybe by asking your visitors to fill in a questionnaire or just talking to them.

Did the people you expected actually come ?

Had they seen your adverts /press release/posters or heard by word of mouth?

✳ Although this is written in business jargon (which this book tries to avoid) the philosophy outlined can be applied to a small craft business just as well as a big business.

Marketing

Did they buy the work you expected them to?

Were they satisfied with the product?

Did they have any useful comments, which might result in improvements being made?

Try to learn from them as they are your bread and butter and they need to be happy to recommend you, **as word of mouth is the very best and cheapest way of advertising.**

Possible targets for improved public relations:

- increasing your mailing list,

- holding open days,

- making a new one-off piece each month,

- improving facilities e.g.to provide visitors coffee.

Anything which makes the customer feel valued and provides opportunities for them to view your work in a peaceful and comfortable setting.

If you're selling designs which will remain static for a while it may be worth investing in a catalogue. This can be a cost effective marketing tool as you can include information about yourself, your business plus images of the actual items on sale. An all in one piece of advertising - but plan how to circulate them first.

Marketing techniques
for visual artists and craftspeople

Run by an established and well known contemporary gallery this course offers a practical guide to marketing and promotion.
Learn the skills to increase the awareness of your businesss and therefore your sales.

The Ferrers Gallery achieved the Silver Award for Marketing Excellence.

Ferrers Gallery, Staunton Harold,
Ashby de la Zouch,,
Leicestershire,
LE65 1RU

Tel 01332 863337
Open Tues - Sun 11am - 5pm
Visit www.ferrersgallery.co.uk

e-mail info@ferrersgallery.co.uk

CONTEMPORARY BRITISH CRAFT AND APPLIED AR

Marketing by Rachael Chambers

Rachael Chambers, who owns and runs the Ferrers Gallery also runs courses on marketing for visual artists and craftspeople, has kindly written the following piece giving her tips on a good marketing campaign. She endorses many of the suggestions given elsewhere in this book.

Marketing is an integral part of your business. Marketing is often thought of as just a promotional activity, but it is actually fundamental to your business and should begin when you decide to set up your business. Marketing should influence many of your business decisions and begin when you are deciding the basics of your business activities such as the products you produce and the price you sell for, the people you sell to, the place you sell from and how you promote your work to your potential customers.

Research

In the initial stages of setting up your business you will need to do a lot of research to find out if there is a market for your work. You will need to look at your competitors. Competitors will be other craftspeople in your field as well as craftspeople in general. In fact anyone who is also vying for your customers money. You will need to find out as much as you can about their business activities to ensure you are different to them. What you are looking for is your Unique Selling Point (USP), something that makes you different from the

Marketing by Rachael Chambers

rest. For example, can you make things to a higher standard, at a more reasonable price or is your product completely different to anyone else in the market?

Customers

Once you have researched the competition and found your USP you will need to look at who might buy your products. Where they live, what their lifestyle is like, what magazines and newspapers they read, what disposable income they have, what they do in their spare time and what they spend their money on. All this information will help lead you to making calculated decisions on where, when and to whom you promote.

For example you may find your customer base is affluent couples aged 40-60 who live locally, they enjoy walking, dining and fine wines and enjoy travelling and days out. They enjoy spending their money on their homes and themselves now that their children are adults themselves and no longer live with them. You may have several different types of customers, don't forget galleries are also a customer.

You will need to decide which group will give you the greatest return on your investment, ie. the time and money you may spend on targeting this audience against the possible sales you could gain.

If you know people that fall into these categories personally question them about their lifestyle and habits and show them your products to see whether they are

Marketing by Rachael Chambers

interested and what they would be willing to pay.

Does this allow you to make a profit? If it doesn't then you will need to think again about your product and how you make it. Many craftspeople go into business because they enjoy what they are doing but don't really think about the pricing of their products and soon go out of business because they got their pricing wrong. (See also the section on pricing p100).

It may be expensive and difficult to target the affluent couples as they travel a lot and read the quality glossies, but their disposable income is much greater than other customers might be so is it worth promoting to them? You may have a customer type that is much easier to reach but doesn't spend quite as much. You will need to decide who is going to give you the greatest return on your investment.

Galleries

Galleries are a good target market as they are easy to reach and can give a good return as they will want to purchase several items at once but they will want to buy at trade prices so your mark up won't be as great as selling direct. When approaching a gallery you need to think about the following:

- Make sure you have a good collection of work to promote to a gallery.

Marketing by Rachael Chambers

- Make sure you are confident in you abilities and can sell your work verbally as well as on paper.

- Have a clear pricing structure for your work.

- Have professional looking marketing materials.

- Make sure you have created your contacts data base and have a named person to see/speak to.

- Visit as many galleries as you can to get a feel for the type of work they sell (Your work will not be suitable for all galleries).

- Don't cold call, you may be disappointed if you have travelled a long way and the buyer or owner isn't in, is too busy or doesn't see cold callers, which many don't.

- If you have galleries near to you call them and arrange an appointment to bring your work to show them. They may want to see imagery and pricing before they agree to meet with you.

- Send galleries a letter introducing yourself and your work and enclose your marketing materials; don't forget the trade price and RRP list.

Marketing by Rachael Chambers

- If you send photos of your work enclose an SAE if you wish these returned to you.

- If you produce small, inexpensive items such as greetings cards consider sending a sample.

- If you are attending any trade fairs or exhibiting in any exhibitions then include details of these. Many gallery owners will want to see your work before placing an order and a trade show is a good way for them to see many potential suppliers in one go.

- Give the gallery a ring after a few days to see that they have received your marketing materials.

- Don't be disappointed if you don't get a reply, some galleries will keep your work on file for future reference or your work may not be suitable for that gallery.

- Keep looking for new galleries/outlets for your work and send them your marketing materials.

- Keep your marketing materials up to date.

- Do keep existing contacts up to date with any change in your details, products or attendance at trade shows or events.

Marketing by Rachael Chambers

Where to sell?

Once you have established your customer profiles you should consider how you might sell to them.

Will you sell from home; the internet or have a work-shop or studio that your customers can visit?

Will you attend craft fairs or sell through galleries? You might decide to do a mixture of these, but your potential customers should influence this decision i.e. if they are likely to prefer buying direct from the maker or purchasing via a gallery.

Now you are clear on your product, your pricing, the place where you will be selling from and the people you are targeting you can look at promotional activities.

Because of the research you have done this process shouldn't be quite so daunting or as expensive as it would have been.

Promotional Activities

Having looked at the lifestyles of your customers, you will note things that they do, read or visit etc. From this you will need to look at how you might reach them through these activities. Promotion doesn't just mean adverts in the local newspaper. Think about other options such as postcards or leaflets delivered direct to your customers homes, posters in health clubs, adverts in national craft magazines, leaflets in arts and tourist venues, talks about your work to women's guilds, information packs to gallery owners. Promotion doesn't

Marketing by Rachael Chambers

need to be expensive, just targeted. Don't fall in the trap of producing a leaflet but not distributing it.

Make sure you time your promotional activities carefully so you are able to take on any increased workload resulting from extra sales and that you target your customers when they are likely to be interested. Summer is a good time to target the tourists but not the locals as they maybe away too.

Think carefully about your message, and think back to your USP, it is this you will need to focus on and promote for it is this that will make you stand out from the crowd. With visual arts and crafts an image is the strongest promotional tool as it is often the aesthetics of your product that your customers will be appreciating. Your visual identity is an important part of the professional outlook you are establishing. You may decide to have a logo created by a graphic designer or you may choose the same typeface throughout your promotional materials to help create this identity.

Promotional materials need not be expensive if thought about carefully. **The one expense that is critical to your success is the photography**. This should be done professionally as good photography is imperative to the promotion of your work. Poor photography will not show your work at it's best.

Get your photographer to take photos of the whole of a piece of work as well as closer detail photos. Choose to take photos on a plain white background so that

Marketing by Rachael Chambers

photos can be 'cut outs' or cropped to suit. By doing this in one shoot you have many more options to work with.

Request the copyright for the photographs. This way they can be used in the future, you don't have to get copyright for every photograph, just the ones you like.

Do agree a price for the photo shoot in advance. Be clear what this includes i.e. number of items to be photographed, number of prints, copyright costs, images on a disk etc. Once you have some photography to work with you will need to think of the design. Think also of ways you can design your artwork to allow for changes and additions:

- Make sure it looks professional; consider employing a graphic designer if you are not confident in your own skills

- Think of how a catalogue might be bound so that additions can be added or kept as loose sheets

- Get someone to design your publicity material for use on your computer so you can print out things as you need them. Do separate sheets for things that may change, such as prices.

- If you are going to move or change your contact details in the near future be careful what you publish it on or it will date very quickly.

Press Releases by Rachael Chambers

- Make sure everything is included; imagery, prices, contact details, your inspiration and techniques, delivery terms, minimum order etc.

Professional printing is not imperative but will give the right impression – it need not be expensive in fact it may even be more cost effective than making packs yourself.

You might not need to do all you marketing materials professionally but you could consider doing your business cards, letterheads, postcards, or a folder or catalogue. With digital technology printing prices for small quantities is much more cost effective.

Postcards also eliminate the need for envelopes and do give an instant impression. You can always do a series of photographs to show your collection and there is no reason why several images can't be used on one postcard.

You could also have stickers printed; these can seal your envelopes, go on packaging materials or on folders. When you have produced your marketing materials, make them cost effective by using them to bring in sales. Marketing materials however well produced are no good left in a box.

You will need to create a database of contacts, including galleries, good customers etc. This will take time and a bit of research but it will be worth it. Don't forget to find the buyers or owners name at the gallery.

Press Releases by Rachael Chambers

Media Coverage

Media coverage can be the most cost effective means of promoting your business. It will take time and effort but you can reap your rewards in raising your profile. It is however a bit "hit and miss" in that you cannot guarantee the coverage. For guaranteed exposure you will need to go with paid advertising. To increase your chances of inclusion here are a few guidelines:

1. Have a clear, powerful or intriguing title. The reporter will receive many press releases each day – yours needs to stand out from the crowd.

2. Make sure you have something to tell.

3. Use a clear typeface such as Arial, using an unusual typeface will make it hard for the reader to decipher the information and it may be discarded before they get past the title.

4. Line space the text to at least 1.5 spacing, so that the reporter can write notes in between the lines.

5. Make sure you have all the what, where, why and when's detailed in the main body of the text.

6. Don't waffle on. If something needs further explanation then attach a separate sheet.

7. Include the date and 'for immediate release' or add an embargo (don't publish until) date and time, if appropriate.

Press Releases by Rachael Chambers

8. Don't use technical language but write in plain English. Unless for specialist press. Include details of a photo opportunity if relevant.

9. Don't use abbreviations or acronyms.

10. Think about the paper/magazine you are sending the press release to and write it in their style.

11. Always write in the third person.

12. Do include a quote, it can be from you or from someone else. If it is from someone else such as a customer gain their permission first.

13. Finish the release with the words 'ends'. And then follow with your contact details or photo opportunity suggestions. This is so the reporter knows where the text ends and where additional information, not for print, begins.

14. Do send a good quality photo, if relevant, with information regarding the photo on the back (Tip; write on a sticky label and put on the back of the photo to save writing showing through). Do not send photos to radio contacts!

15. Put in an invitation to an event if this is relevant.

16. Check all dates and telephone numbers, always spell check your press release and get someone else to read through it to check for any errors or omissions.

Press Releases by Rachael Chambers

Writing the press release is only part of the process, sending it is equally as important.

1. Send your press release and photo by email if possible – it means the reporter can lift the text making their job easier, but do make sure you have a title to the email which will make them want to open it otherwise it may get binned immediately.

2. If posting your press release consider printing it on coloured or unusual paper and using a coloured envelope. You may want to handwrite the envelope, as reporters are always getting mail with computer generated sticky labels. They may open a handwritten envelope first.

3. Do spend some time researching possible publications, radio & T.V. stations and you need to find out contact details but also find a name to send it to. Ring them up and find out who does the arts pages, business pages or listings then request their email address too.

4. Check publication lead times-regional and national magazines have at least a three month lead time.

5. Don't send local press releases this far in advance their lead times are usually a few weeks or even days and they will forget you sent it.

Marketing by Rachael Chambers

6. Do however send details of events as soon as you know of them to local radio & T.V. stations, tourist information centres and tourist boards as they often have a web-site detailing events for the forthcoming year.

7. Don't forget to send your press release to regional agencies and arts organisations. They often have newsletters, but do find out the full contact details as you would for other press.

8. Be realistic don't send your press release to every publication you know of–just the ones you feel will be interested in your story. Each time you send a press release this list may be different.

9. Get to know the contacts at publications, this way you can ring them to tell them that there is a press release on its way that will interest them. It means they will be looking out for it. (Some national paper reporters will receive in excess of 100 press releases a day)

10. Don't expect every publication or radio station to publish or broadcast your story.

Evaluation

Keep a record of all the media coverage and marketing activities you do as you will need to evaluate their effectiveness. The best way to do this is to ask your customers how they heard about you and your business, what they thought of the promotional materials, where

Marketing by Rachael Chambers

they came from, what they like and what they purchased along with any general comments made.

Evaluate your marketing activities on a regular basis to determine what is or isn't working and make the appropriate changes to the activities you do in the future. To re-cap-a good press release should be: concise (maximum two pages), well written; factual, honest and timely.

Awards

Awards are a great way to gain media coverage and prestige. There are awards for your products, your business activities etc. Look out for them in industry newsletters, magazines, and newspapers. If you are short listed or win then shout about it!!

In fact you should be shouting about and promoting your business whenever and wherever you are–many a commission has come through a conversation with a stranger at a dinner party.

Some useful websites for more advice and examples:
www.pressbox.co.uk
www.ereleases.com
www.scottishenterprise.com
www.aimhigher.ac.uk

ferrers gallery

The award winning Ferrers Gallery promotes the very best in British Contemporary Craft and Applied Arts. Situated in an old granary in the picturesque Valley of Staunton Harold the gallery sells jewellery, textiles, glass, ceramics, metalwork and paintings and has a year round exhibition programme.

Ferrers Gallery, Staunton Harold,
Ashby de la Zouch,,
Leicestershire,
LE65 1RU

Tel 01332 863337
Open Tues - Sun 11am - 5pm
Visit www.ferrersgallery.co.uk
e-mail info@ferrersgallery.co.uk

CONTEMPORARY BRITISH CRAFT AND APPLIED ARTS

Planning

BCF Books office

Planning

✳ 'Planning is an unnatural process – it is much more fun to do something. The nicest thing about not planning is that failure comes as a complete surprise, rather than being preceded by a period of worry and depression.'

This quote is attributed to Sir John Harvey-Jones, a very successful business tycoon. It is reassuring he agrees that planning is vital. It is essential to take control of your business, however small it is, so that you do not lurch from emergency to emergency. It is tempting to just deal with the pleasant tasks and spend time working at your craft.

It has been pointed out that successful people are those who make it a habit to do the things which failures don't like doing. They don't like doing accounts, filing etc. but know they have to be done for the business to run smoothly.

For good **time management** you need a clear idea of what you are trying to achieve, your aims and objectives. You have already calculated how much work you need to sell in order to make the minimum turnover. If you are continuing with a part-time job, whilst you get your business established, this will obviously allow you to build up the business gradually.

✳ A quote well worth thinking about.

Planning

Three Year Plan

It will help you to plan your objectives if you set out a three year plan, divided into monthly sections and possibly sub-divided (at least at the start) into weekly tasks. This will help you clarify what you hope to achieve by certain times and outline how to succeed.

At the start the goals will probably include setting up a workshop, buying necessary equipment - perhaps over a period of six months. If you are working from home you may be still purchasing the equipment but also building up some savings, towards a future workshop. Listing your aims for where you want your work to be sold i.e. in two trade shows and three galleries by the end of the first year, will also help you to focus.

By year two you will wish to have built up your sales through finding more galleries to take your work and perhaps being selected for a prestigious show, like the Chelsea Craft Fair (now at Somerset House). At the same time moving your marketing plan forward to spread the word about your product and maybe having a private exhibition.

By year three you should aim to be achieving your estimated turnover by selling steadily through X no of galleries, have a regular circuit of shows to attend plus a couple of expensive commissions.

Planning

At the beginning of each week look at all that has to be done. You may find it useful to give yourself a daily task list. An urgent order may come in one day and cause you to re-schedule a whole day. You can just re-list the tasks in order of priority and all will get done, with no panic.

It is important to make your lists realistic and therefore achievable, you will then have a great feeling of satisfaction, as you cross things off, rather than being stressed at an inability to keep up with your own targets. When researching a particular project, e.g. finding new galleries, give yourself a written list of those to investigate, you can then tick off those dealt with and keep a record of results. Even if you get disturbed you will know where you are and not have to try and carry the information in your head.

(Lists help to clear the mind)

By having a definite plan of action it is easier to say ✳ no to something that may be suggested. If you can see that it will not help you progress to your goal, you don't want to waste time.

Another useful piece of advice which I read in a business magazine was to remember to take regular five minute breaks. If you were part of a team or working in

✳ Trying to deal with the worst task of the day first and learning to say 'No' are two useful points to remember.

Planning

an office these would happen naturally, social chat with a colleague or at a scheduled coffee break.

❊ Working on your own you still need to stop, walk around, make a short private phone call, have a drink. You will return to work much fresher and achieve more than by plodding on hour after hour. Even if you really enjoy your creative work a break really is essential.

Apart from your main creative craftwork and essential day to day administrative work you should remember to keep time to update your Portfolio/Self Promotion kit. It is important to do this regularly so that your CV is always ready to send out and recent images are available, saved on your computer at the right dpi, to send out with publicity whenever required. I have been surprised that some, apparently professional makers, have been unable to provide me with recent images for a publication. I imagined they would have been prepared and felt this showed a serious failure of 'planning' i.e. thinking ahead.

Finally, try to progamme in time for thinking and creating new designs on paper, as you need to keep your work fresh. This is a luxury which you had at University but will never have again - unless you plan for it.

❊ Regular breaks really will help you work better; although it is tempting to keep on and on , particularly when in the middle of an engrossing task.

Business Plan

The Actual Business Plan

Although this sounds an alarming challenge it is quite straight forward and will be a very useful tool. From this plan your prospective funder (bank /grant giver etc.) should be able to see exactly **what** you plan to do or make and **How and what** your business aims are for the next year three years. The plan should be as realistic as possible and will provide something to relate to when you monitor your progress in the future.

The business plan should include the following:

- **Personal details:**
  Name/Address: Limited Company Number/ Partnership/Sole Trader (see p158)
  What the Business does and date it started trading or plans to start. Possibly include images of some of your work.

- Your **CV** and a list of any other people who will be working in the business and their roles.

- ❋ **Mission statement with aims and objectives** for a minimum of three years.

❋ Mission statement sounds impressive - but it just means your hopes for what the business will achieve.

Business Plan

Market research results, to prove there is a market for your product and at what price you plan to be selling your work. Catalogue or Price list if you have one.

- Your **marketing plan** to show what methods you plan to use to achieve sales.

  A "SWOT Analysis" showing your business strengths, weaknesses, opportunities and threats.

- **Premises** giving details about your workshop, shared studio etc. or explain that you will be working from home.

The funder will need to know if it is freehold or leasehold, with details of rent or mortgage (who will be responsible for repairs in and out etc.) plus a valuation. The size of the premises, what area is to be used for work. Does it need any redesigning/decorating to suit your needs Is it in the right **location**?

- **Equipment,** list any you may already have (with money owed if relevant) and proposed new purchases. If any thing needs to be hired, list this too.

- **Finances,** a summary of what money is needed to start up and then to keep the business running until sufficient income comes in to take over the running costs.

Business Plan

- **Cash Flow Forecast** This will show how the cash is flowing in, from sales, salary (if relevant) and funding and flowing out, to cover running and living expenses.

- **Own investment** A statement of how much money you will be putting in yourself and any grants you may already have. Also any other income you will have from teaching etc. Most funders prefer the applicant to have raised at least half the finances themselves.
  (see Grants p280)

- **Monitoring Plan,** this will show your funder that you have a plan in hand to keep a close check on how their finances are being used.

A funder's decision to lend or not will depend very much on how convincing your market research has been in showing that there really is a need for what you intend doing. You need to satisfy them (and yourself) that you have studied the market and know that there is not only potential for business to start with but in the future too. A lender has to feel confident that you can pay back his loan. You may have amazing ideas but if they are not realistic; if the figures do not add up to provide sufficient income to pay you and also to pay him, he is unlikely to take you on.

Business Plan

Your funder may ask for security, in other words he wants some collateral against things going wrong and his payments not being made. A relative might agree to be a security for you or, if you own some other property perhaps this can be used as collateral security.

It is recognised that most new businesses run into trouble during their first few years as the cash doesn't flow. ✳ Do not under estimate the amount you need to borrow. When you have done all your sums and written all the charts, you still may have forgotten that although you hope to have sold 20 items by the end of month 1, the chances are that you wont' be paid for them all until well into month two. Meanwhile all the everyday bills still need paying and your funds are going down. So make sure you allow for unforeseen situations (which can be included in your budget) and seek a large enough loan on your initial application.

One bank drew attention to the point that if you seek funds, to buy a particular piece of equipment, be sure that the terms allow the loan to be paid off, before the life expectancy of the equipment has ended. Also beware of early redemption charges and penalties for early redemption.

✳ The majority of businesses start up with private money, from family or friends. Never under estimate how much you will need - it will always be more than you have calculated on paper.

Business Plan

The Cash Flow is a vital part of the plan (and possibly the most difficult to put on paper). You can write a synopsis of your cash flow as a mix of text and figures, simply explaining exactly what your setting up costs are likely to be (running through the headings already mentioned here). Then outlining how you expect to cover the costs and how much you are hoping to borrow to include a margin for the unexpected.

It is all to do with profit and loss, not cash. You should include any item that gives a profit or is a cost against profit. Do not include any other items, such as capital expense, if they will not directly affect your profits.

Writing out a Cash Flow. Although the figures will be estimated in most cases, helps you to see how your business might develop.✳ It may reveal glaring errors in your planning, if so now is the time to take advice from an expert and see if there is some way around the problem. Better to see it on paper now than for it to happen in real life The Cash Flow also provides a record to check against as the business progresses, a quick way to see if you are on target.

When calculating your cash flow decide on the credit period which you plan to grant your customers. The usual is 30 days, so if you deliver some work to a gallery

✳ The budgeting exercise is a useful planning tool.

Business Plan

in mid-February, with an invoice for £250, you must remember that £250 will not appear in your account until mid March (if you are lucky). It can be difficult to keep buyers up to the mark on settling accounts.If you are not reclaiming VAT (and it is unlikely that you will be registered at this stage) you must still include the VAT element of your expenses, as you will not get it back, it will therefore affect your projected profit.

List all your expected income on a **monthly basis,** giving a ✳ total at the end of each column. Then list all your anticipated expenses, also month by month with totals. It is easy to read one off against the other and get a picture of how the profit or loss is flowing.

Example of items Expenses column:

The type of things which will appear in your list of expenses are similar to those listed in the Business Overheads in Pricing (see page 101). Plus extra setting up costs and loan repayments, don't forget to include an amount for 'drawings' this means the amount you are allowing yourself for wages.

Example of items for income column:

In the income columns include anticipated sales, any fees you expect to receive, extra salary from part-time work (perhaps as a teacher), any savings you may already have plus any grants /loans you have in place

✳ Negative totals are shown in brackets.

Business Plan

Example for a month:

If your estimated expenses total £2,200 and your income totals £1,450 you have a shortfall of £750. However if you work out the figures for each month you will hope to see a positive balance. Some months you will be earning more from sales, other months your salary may be coming in etc. By checking the estimated figures you can see if the business has a realistic chance of survival. You can also see how much you really need to borrow to start it off. As has been emphasised be sure to give yourself enough to create a buffer against the lean times, without making the repayment fees so enormous, that you cannot keep them up.

Take professional advice before committing yourself but if you plan to use an accountant do get an estimate of their charges first.

Some technical explanations:

If you are working towards a ✳ bank loan you may have a form including a few disconcerting words and phrases. These three all mean the same '**variable costs**' '**direct costs**' or '**cost of sales**', the latter is self explanatory. They are referring to all costs incurred in producing your product, raw materials and any wages.

✳ Most high street banks have free comprehensive leaflets about setting up a new business, which will probably take you through the Business Plan exercise.

Business Plan

'Indirect costs', 'expenses', 'overheads' and 'fixed costs' also all mean the same - they are the costs of rent, rates, heating, insurance, salaries (including your own draw-ings, money for daily living) etc.

Depreciation is another word used in operating budgets, meaning loss of value of stock/equipment etc. It also includes writing off capital items for tax purposes.

Monitoring

The Business Plan should be followed and an accounts system set up to make it easy to check monthly figures. In this way you can check back, against your estimated figures, and detect any major differences. This should alert you to any future problems, before they occur. It is a good idea to get into the habit of updating your cash flow forecasts, to keep on top of the financial situation.

Although the planning quote by Sir John Harvey Jones (p85) is amusing, it is pointing out how important it is to look ahead and check sales figures so that you are warned if trouble is brewing, however unpleasant this may be.

www.artquest.org.uk

This site has already been mentioned but as it appears to be a comprehensive source of advice (which is also regularly updated) for anyone setting up a business it is worth emphasising its importance.

Financial

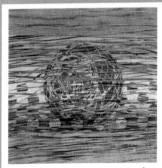

NEIL BOTTLE DESIGNS

Pricing by Chris Noble

Frosty Morning - Original limited edition digital print
by Chris Noble

Pricing by Chris Noble

Chris Noble: *Craftsman/printmaker and Lecturer in Professional Practice to BA Design Crafts and BA Blacksmith students at Herefordshire College of Art. For years a director of the Lion Gallery, Leominster.*

Many young craftspeople find that pricing their work is one of the biggest headaches they encounter when first setting up. However good the quality of the finished items and the publicity promotion may be, not understanding the way it should be priced can rapidly lead to the collapse of a new business.

There are many ways to cost individual and batch products, mostly complex and more suited to a much larger business with their teams of accountants and managers. The individual craftsperson needs a simple and foolproof method of covering all the costs incurred in making, together with the built in profit element.

One starting point is to go out and about to research what others are charging for similar items on sale in galleries and shops all over the country. This will help give the 'feel' for the right price bracket which the work naturally falls into.

Galleries, in different locations, urban and rural, will have different mark-ups as their own costs will vary enormously, together with their perception of what their customers will pay for a given item. But to only use this method is problematic since the galleries own costs and mark-ups are hidden, as are the maker's own

Pricing by Chris Noble

costs. In other words you cannot tell what an individual's costs are likely to be just by looking at the finished product; are they married to a rich lawyer, do they have a free workshop at home, do they buy their materials efficiently? Crucially, are they making a decent profit?

So looking at other people's pricing serves only as a guideline to see if the final price appears to be viable. What is needed is a more thorough costing method which means sitting down and collecting some vital figures together. Sometimes this can be a painful business, confronting reality early on, but it will be worth it in the long run.

The price tag in the gallery covers a number of costs which must be met. Firstly there will be the gallery's own✳ mark-up or commission which may account for up to 50% of the retail price. The rest is the wholesale price which goes to cover all the costs of the maker. These include:

the materials, the costs of making, the costs of running the business, personal drawings and lastly a percentage for profit.

✳ This issue is discussed in more depth in the galleries section see page 170 and at the end of this piece on page 110.

Pricing by Chris Noble

This simple analysis shows up some important points, for when a craftsperson intends to work full time, making a living entirely from their sales, it is clear that all the costs of running the business, together with all their own personal drawings (can be thought of as wages), must come from the accumulated sales income. To get a little more technical it comes down to apportioning the level of recovery of the costs involved in the business overheads and the maker's labour.

What is meant by Business Overheads?

Basically any business has costs for it to exist at all. These may include:

rent, business rates, utility charges (gas, electricity, water), telephone bills, repairs and maintenance, equipment and tools, hire charges, transport costs, postage, packaging, fees for solicitors, accountants and professional advice, stationery, advertising and printing, bank charges, general consumable items (everything from sellotape to drawing pins), and just about everything else that a business uses.

Note, however, that not one of these items listed makes you any money, they simply add up to the expenses incurred in running practically any business. Typically for a small craft business the figures could look like the sample list on next page:

Pricing by Chris Noble

Rent	£1,800
Rates	£600
Insurance	£250
Vehicle/fuel	£900
Utilities (gas & electricity)	£250
Telephone	£300
General materials	£500
Accountant and legal	£400
Tools and equipment	£400
Postage	£60
Stationery	£180
Bank Charges	£75
Repairs and renewals	£90
Depreciation (£2000 over 4 years)	£500
Miscellaneous items (disposable items such as rags, bleach, sellotape etc.)	£80

Total   Overhead   £6,385

Personal drawings

These cover all the private expenses in day to day living and keeping a roof over your head. Not only:
all food, clothing, travel, holidays but rent or mortgage, gas and electricity bills, entertainment, children, pets, presents, gardening etc..

Pricing by Chris Noble

In fact all the money you don't spend on the business but spend on yourself and any family you have comes under personal drawings. A young craftsperson's personal drawings audit might look like this:

Mortgage	£3,600
Rates and council tax	£900
Food bill	£2,650
Clothing	£450
Vehicle/fuel	£800
Household goods	£450
Leisure/entertainment	£650
Holiday	£750
Pet	£135
Utilities	£700
Telephone	£320
Miscellaneous items	£275

Total personal expenses £11,080

It is time to sit down and calculate just how much you do expect to spend in a year on yourself and running your business. You need to do an annual audit if you like, and it is not as difficult as it sounds. Gathering all the weekly shopping bills, all the utility bills, the regular outgoing monthly and quarterly payments and putting them down on paper will eventually give you a total expected annual expenditure for the year-an estimate

Pricing by Chris Noble

but based on sound and predictable evidence.

Now you need to do just the same to calculate the expected annual expenditure on the business overheads. Get quotes if necessary and be sensible. What will the annual gas or electricity bill be if you are a potter and a heavy user of either or both?

The more detailed the figures the more accurate your predictions will be and allow for inflation where necessary. So now you should have two annual figures for personal drawings and business overheads. Leave aside the main materials used for the moment, we will come back to them later.

Another calculation is now needed to put these figures to use. You need to ask yourself how many hours are you going to work in an average week? Be honest here; are you really going to work nine to five, six days a week?

Many crafts people do work 48 hours a week or more but can you keep it up all year? Realistically you need to consider:

Lunch breaks, phone calls, delivery trips, holidays, marketing expeditions, research, trips to the bank, the post office, clearing up, dealing with visitors and customers, all of which prevent you from making, and importantly it is only when you are making that you can be earning as a result.

There is plenty of research to show that, from your eight hours a day, you will be lucky to be actually

Pricing by Chris Noble

creating saleable work during five of those hours. In fact you will be likely to only make for 24 hours a week out of a forty hour working week. It will vary from person to person but it's important to be honest with yourself.

It is only from the hours during which you make that any income can be derived:
a working year of 48 weeks (allowing for holidays and illness) making for 24 hours a week will only give you a total of 1,152 hours a year.

Those 1,152 hours are the only hours that are going to provide income.

Now back to the two annual totals calculated earlier. It is useful to work out your hourly rates. To work out an hourly rate, to cover all your overheads, divide the business overheads by the number of hours available. To work out the hourly rate to cover all your personal drawings, divide that total by the number of hours available. You can combine the two rates to make one but it is useful to have the two rates for other calculations later. Using the figures from earlier, the overhead hourly rate would be:

£6,385 divided by 1,152 hours=£5.54 an hour

The personal drawings rate would be:
£11,080 divided by 1,152 hrs=£9.62 an hour

Pricing by Chris Noble

To calculate the price of a single item you need to keep an accurate record of how long it takes to make, say in this case five hours. The calculation would go like this:

Five hours x business overhead rate @ £5.54 = £27. 70

Five Hours x personal drawing rate @ £9.62 = £48.10
Materials used specifically for an item £14
                                            Total = £89.80

Add percentage for profit, say 25% @ £22.45= **£112.25**

**This is the wholesale figure probably rounded up
for simplicity to £113 or even £115.**

One side result of this is that you will have to keep a good record of how long things take to make to be able to price them accurately, and that is a good discipline to get into.

If you make a single standard item then life is fairly simple:. In this case divide the number of hours available by the time it takes to make each single item. Thus 1,152 divided by five will mean you can make about 231 in a year to cover all of your costs and make a profit. (Total potential revenue value of £25,929.75). In most cases, however, you will be making a range of products including many one-off items which will need to be costed as above every time. So it becomes very obvious

Pricing by Chris Noble

that you always need to make full use of your available time - **time, in this case, really is money.** Generating a profit is important. It will see you through the lean times and give you something to set aside for retiring or re-investing in new equipment, a bigger workshop or whatever. The profit element is flexible and gives you a margin to shave and adjust to ensure that crucially the price remains viable. This is where your research on prices generally will become helpful.

With all the separate elements calculated you have powerful tools to analyse:

- *How the business is going; will it break even?*

- *How much profit will you make this year or next?*

- *How many individual items do you need to sell to meet all your costs?*

The concept of ✳ **break even** is an important one because before you have covered all your costs, materials and paid yourself you are not actually making any profit. So although you have built in a profit margin per item, selling that one item does not make you that profit alone.

✳ Although some people may be put off by all this talk of break even point and the Contribution etc. do persevere. This article explains very clearly how the pricing structure work, **it is essential reading.**

Pricing by Chris Noble

You have to pay for all your overheads out of sales and that is done at a particular cost in terms of materials and your labour. So to ensure you have really covered all your overheads you will have spent money on materials and paying yourself to live. Only when you have covered all your overheads can you begin to make a profit.

To understand this it is helpful to think in terms of the contribution each item makes to covering the costs as follows:

Wholesale price minus costs to produce (total labour and materials) this gives a figure called the Contribution, which is made up from the overhead hourly rate total and the added profit figure. These contributions go towards paying for your business overheads firstly and then when that is covered become the contributions towards the final profit.

The point at which the change over occurs is called the **break even** point - that is neither a loss or profit is being made. To survive you must reach this point or have borrowing lined up to tide you over until such time as you do. Only when you go past this point can a profit be generated.

The great art is to piece together a year's production that ensures you meet the required targets you have set yourself and pays for all that projected spending. Working out the contribution of each item will help you achieve this.

Pricing by Chris Noble

Finally it is necessary to be viable, meaning that the work you produce looks as if it is worth the amount being charged. An egg cup that took six weeks to make and cost £2,000 would not be viable, but a small table might be. The ability to negotiate on price is useful but does mean you need to know, inside out, your own pricing structure, to know if you can afford to give a 10% discount for a bulk order or cash on delivery.

Some other details worth considering include: *pricing design time separately, perhaps at a lower rate, pricing commissions in a way that ensures you don't lose out on delivery and installation.*

When costing materials it pays to add a contingency say 10%, to cover wastage and inflation. Materials which are impossible to cost per item such as glue or thread or nails and screws need to be added into your general overhead costs and be recouped during the year.

If you intend to sell direct to customers you will need your own retail price rather than just selling at the wholesale figure. You may arrive at this by adding say 80% to the wholesale figure to achieve a price that is reasonable when compared to the full retail price that a gallery may have to charge but not undercutting them by so much as to upset them. Remember selling direct involves more of your time and has its own expenses to be accounted for.

Pricing by Chris Noble

Pricing for Sale or Return

Many makers fail to understand the difference between mark-up and commission; essential when dealing with SOR

Mark-up-if a gallery buys your work outright at the wholesale price they will very likely double the figure - that is 'mark it up' by 100%. So If you supply an item at £40 they will sell it for £80 (possibly + VAT too).

With SOR it is best to set the retail price (in this case £80) from which they will take their commission.

Commission can vary from 25% to 45% but is very often about 40%. In this case when the item sells they would take £36 and you would receive £44. You get a slightly higher rate but will have to wait for the item to sell as the gallery has not taken the risk of putting its own money upfront. Generally you should seek to maintain a constant retail price from outlet to outlet regardless of whether they are buying or having work on SOR.

As mentioned in the Galleries section you must discuss prices with your gallery and come to an agreement, if possible that you will not undercut their selling price when/if selling direct yourself.

alison branagan

creative consultancy

Creative Industry Specialist

For information about workshops consultancy & enterprise support

visit www.alisonbranagan.com
contact alison@alisonbranagan.com
phone +44 (0) 20 8365 0453

Illustrations George Lincoln © 2004
Website by www.virtuallee.co.uk

Getting Paid by Alison Branagan

Alison Branagan who runs her own business as a creative consultant, established courses and gives one to one advice. (adverts on page 138) Alison has written this section highlighting the finer points of getting paid; possibly the most important part of business.

When you are researching and preparing for business you should discover how your clients or customers would expect to pay you. Many designers deal with cheques, cash and credit card transactions at retail craft or design fairs. Others rely on business cheques and electronic payments from firms, agents, and arts organisations, upon presentation of invoices.

The majority of payment problems occur between designers and their clients due to the lack of clear agreements in the early stage of commission or order. For example, verbal agreements, made without proper contracts being in place before the designer starts work, can lead to misunderstandings and confusion later on.

This quick seven-step guide below will assist you in setting up payment procedures.

1. Professional Presentation

Make sure your business stationary, cards and documents are of a high standard. When you are giving receipts, using carbon receipt books are OK, but it is better to have properly printed books with your business name, design format or branding incorporated.

Getting Paid by Alison Branagan

✳ If issuing invoices or order forms ensure that they are printed on high quality letterheads. This aids in giving a good impression of your business to the customer.

2. Letters of agreements, order forms and contracts
Confirming agreements for commissions or delivery of products/services can clarify the payment structure, e.g. £% up front, or on delivery, or at agreed stages.

3. Terms and conditions
These are very important and will save you from future disagreements if Terms and Conditions are invested in at an early stage. To get an idea have a look on other design companies' websites, under 'Legal' or 'T&C', this will give you an idea; they are quite costly to get drawn up, and you need to see an IP solicitor. Terms and conditions are attached to acceptance of commissions, accompanying your letters of agreement, order forms and accessed via your website. They cover many areas and include issues such as payment, rejection or cancellation fees and copyright.

✳ A-N have templates for estimates etc
A5 duplicate, numbered invoice pads (including your branding and design format) are not expensive, approx £35 for 150 invoices from my local printers. Ed

Getting Paid by Alison Branagan

4. Invoicing

An invoice is a bill, which you send to a client or business for work done or at agreed stages within a project. It needs to be on your letter headed paper, numbered, e.g. first one will be numbered '0001'. You need to make sure it is dated, the clients name is on it, details of the order or commission days, hours, services or products made, '20 stripey yellow embroidered cotton cushion covers 45 x 45 cm'. Include the date and year of delivery of the products or services and your terms and conditions. Remember you need to make sure that the client/customer is in agreement with them before hand.

It is good practice to put your self-employment number on the invoice, it is a legal requirement if you are a company to put your registration number and also if you are VAT registered to include these details.

You must keep one hard copy version of each invoice sent in your records of trading and the other can be emailed or posted to the client.

5. Receipts

When trading via retail fairs or markets you need to issue receipts. Hand written receipts can get very time consuming to do. If you do plan to give receipts for payments via cash and cheques then you need to find a speedy way of doing so. If you invest in a receipt book with a perforated divide you must remember to make a note of each sale on the stub. Customers often like to have a proper receipt even for small purchases.

Getting Paid by Alison Branagan

Electronic tills are still a rare thing for designers to invest in and are unnecessary to buy unless you take on a retail unit or shop where there will be a large number of customers coming through.

6. Electronic Payments

Whether you plan to take credit card, debit payments or even cheques you need special equipment. To have a credit card processing machine, (known as a PDQ machine) costs a monthly fee plus a % of all sales, you also have to achieve a large minimum turnover. If you are only doing occasional fairs it will not be needed as you will find most will offer a credit card service point, for customers for all the stands. So when you set up your business bank account, talk to your business manager about your needs.

A direct debit is an instruction to your bank to authorise payments from your bigger clients upon a regular basis to your business account, again you need to discuss this with your bank and customer.

To receive payments online via selling from your website you need to have a PSP website know as a Payment Service Provider. You may find your business manger at your bank can help you set up a mercantile payments facility on line. Otherwise organising a 'Pay Pal' or 'World Pay' or 'No Chexs' logo to be placed on your website page (a simpler solution) will offer web users access to buying your products on line, which is really quick and also very low in cost.

Getting Paid by Alison Branagan

7. Late payment

This is the last thing you need in life, but at some point you will find clients or customers who for one reason or another pay late or unfortunately don't pay at all. If you follow the above guidelines and learn more from useful fact sheets ❋ published on UK websites you should find the chances of being placed in this position minimised.

However, what you should do is firstly enquire why something is late before sending reminders and demands for more information; check out some of the useful websites below.

Finally remember the UK is not taking part in the € Euro at the present time, but when invoicing or trading with companies within Europe such as Ireland, or in other parts of the world research into money conversion rates and variation in currency values. Think through how you will sell via your website to overseas buyers.

AB

❋ www.lfyb.lawsociety.org.uk scheme for new business to access free half hour legal advice, use this scheme to get guidance on Terms and Conditions.
www.paypal.com/uk online payment
www.payontime.co.uk free guides and model letters for business on dealing with late payment
www.moneyclaim.gov.uk online court claim service

General accounts

Once your business is up and running you will need to keep a careful check on where the money is going and how much, exactly, is coming in. If you plan to employ an accountant, to help prepare your end of year accounts and tax return, discuss with them the best style of book-keeping for you. If you plan to deal with the accounts yourself, the following may be of help.

Keeping 'the books'

To do this all you need is a very simple accounting system. You can buy 'analysis books' at most good stationers. When I first started a business a useful piece of advice was to choose a book with the maximum number of columns. Although you may not think you need so many, they always come in useful.

Another piece of advice (which I still find difficult to follow) was always find time to sit down and fill in your account books, at least once a week, it is much easier to keep on top of the paperwork if you don't let it accumulate. Therefore check your monthly bank statements against your cheque book as soon as possible each month, it is easy to let it lie in the filing tray waiting for a convenient moment - it will never arrive - just do it.

www.taxassistforsmallbusiness.co.uk
Also has advice about accounts
T: 0800 0523 555

General accounts

Keep all bank records, cheque book stubs and paying in slips, the details can then be copied into your analysis book. In the book, keep one side for Credit, giving columns to record:

- the date of a transaction
- the name of the buyer (if relevant) or just record 'Sale pot 10 ' or the invoice number

- VAT details if relevant

- the date it was paid

- date statement sent if necessary

On the facing page will be many more columns, which you will use for the Debit list. These will be cheque or cash payments made by you. A column for the cheque number, date, name of payee and amount will take up the first three. Then give headings for all that you need, to cover for instance :
Postage, stationery, travel expenses, packaging, rent, rates, insurance, advertising, repairs, equipment, materials, cash drawings etc.
When you fill in the cheque details you then follow across your columns until you find the one relevant and put in the total, this makes end of year accounting very easy. You just add up all the column totals to give annual postage expenses, travel costs etc. If you take a

General accounts

cash sum out of your account to pay petty cash expenses, remember to list, perhaps in a small cash book, what these are, so that you can transfer them to the main book at the end of each week.

You should ✳ keep copies of all your invoices, filed in date order. As they are paid you can take them out and file away. Those that are left unpaid can easily be checked each month, when you need to send out statements. You should also get into the habit of keeping all receipts, they will help to fill in your account book and also may be needed at a later date for the income tax assessments.

When your bank statements arrive, if your books are up to date it should be fairly straight forward to check your total cash flow. Remember to allow for unpaid invoices and work out on SOR.

Stock

To keep track of your stock you should also have a stock book. No doubt makers will evolve their own system to keep a check on stock. A simple way is to give every item that you make a number and list it, with the cost price.

If at a later date you send that item out on SOR you can include the number on your delivery note and then, later still, if it is sold you can record the number on the

✳ You should keep your papers for at least five years.

General accounts

invoice. Eventually when it has been paid for you can cross it off your list, with the amount paid beside it. This way you keep track of all you make, how much each piece actually costs and what profit you have made on which items.

Spreadsheets

If you have access to a computer any simple programme can be used to prepare spreadsheets to layout your accounts. If you have a large enough business, to warrant the initial expense, you may wish to invest in an accounts programme.

You will probably have discussed the type of account you need when you first approach your chosen bank/building society. It is likely to be a business current account, and should provide free banking if you remain in credit. However you may have to negotiate good terms with the manager. A reserve account can also be useful, to save any excess cash (if there is any) and earn a bit of interest. At the time of writing this will be at a very low rate.

Monitoring in general

You will need to monitor your stock, income and expenses closely, particularly during the first few months in order to keep in control.

You also need to consider how the whole business is going, especially if you have benefited from a loan, grant or bursary. Your funder will probably have asked for an evaluation of your performance.

General accounts

If you prepared your Operating Budget and Cashflow Forecasts along the lines that most High Street Banks suggest you will have written an estimated figure for each heading. After, say three months of trading, you can then check the actual figures against the estimated ones to see if you are on target.

It would be amazing if they were an exact match but any large differences should alert you to a possible problem. Perhaps you will find that you have spent more on materials than estimated, because you forgot that you would initially need to buy everything at once, rather than just top up supplies, as you will in the future.

Maybe sales were not as good as you had hoped, due to lack of advertising and you will need to give more time to building your market.

Whatever the problems, if you regularly check your figures you can see if a serious difficulty is arising before it becomes a real disaster. You can then try to do something about it. If in doubt always seek advice from an expert or an experienced trader. It is much better to acknowledge problems rather than sweeping them under the carpet and hoping that they will go away.

It is unlikely that you will be involved with VAT payments in your first few years of trading. You need to know about it as VAT registration is a legal requirement if/when your annual turnover exceeds a declared level of £60,000, in a 12 month period (2006), or you believe

VAT

that the value of the taxable supplies you will make in the next 30 days will ※ exceed £60,000. In which case you must add 17.5% to all your prices. It is possible to make a voluntary registration, if you use a large amount of expensive materials and could benefit from reclaiming the VAT paid on these goods, this would be something to discuss with an accountant or business adviser as it will still involve filling in VAT returns.

As discussed by Chris Noble (p99), when selling through galleries you will need a two tier price list:

a) the wholesale (trade) price at which you can afford to sell to the gallery and on to which they will add their commission.

b) your retail (direct selling) price which should really be the same as the **final** gallery selling price.

If you do not like this attitude you must reconsider whether you wish to sell through galleries and perhaps stick to fairs and other direct selling methods where you cut out the middle man.

Another aspect of pricing which needs to be considered is how to label and list your work. If you are supplying a gallery you will need to supply a duplicated delivery note, which identifies each piece supplied, so

※ www.hmrc.gov.uk.
is the HM Revenue & Customs site which gives all the up to date informatoin about Tax issues.

Paperwork

some form of stock numbering is needed. A simple sticky or tie on tag will be sufficient for the gallery, as they will no doubt provide 'in-house' styled labels for their display.

When the work is delivered, by a carrier or yourself, the gallery will need to check the condition and quantity of the stock against the delivery note and should alert you to any breakages or omissions immediately.

Usually you would invoice the gallery at the same time as delivering the work, and would expect payment to be made within 30 days. Your terms should be printed on your invoice.

If the gallery does not pay within the time limit it is accepted practice to send out a statement (you should check your debtors every month and send out statements), referring them to the previous invoice i.e. giving number, date and amount owed but requiring this to be paid immediately.

Generally the matter will be dealt with quickly but just occasionally you will have to deal with a 'bad debt'. Rachel Gogerly describes her experience on (p216) showing how a quick response to a problem avoided disaster. (see A.Branagan p116)

On one occasion I had to seek help from the Small Claims Court, when a customer refused to respond to statements, calls and polite letters. It is a very simple process, first you fill in forms explaining the debt. Once the County Court have accepted that you are due the

Debtors

money in question they deal with all the paperwork and if necessary send in the bailiff, to claim the money from your customer. It is worth doing a little detective work to check that the customer is still in business, otherwise you may risk losing court expenses plus the debt. As you have to pay for the service, your expenses are added to the claim so if successful you are repaid. However if the court decides that you are not due the money you will have to bere the Court fees so be confident of your position before taking this step.

The Better Payment Practice Group (BPPG) have a website: **www.**payontime.co.uk from which you can download a User's Guide to the Late Payment Act. Probably not necessary for the average small business but if you are into manufacturing it might be useful for dealing with larger companies.

If you are selling your work direct you will need to design your own labels which should be clear and simple giving all the information which a buyer will need.

- Price,

- Not for Sale or Sold ,where relevant,

- Title of work /size (if needed),

- Materials used in the piece,

- What it can be used for-if not obvious,

- Cleaning/care instructions.

Paperwork

It is worth giving time and effort to this small but important detail. If the label is compatible with the material used for the craft it can become an integral part of the whole piece. This eye for detail may attract the attention of and then impress the prospective buyer.

Some of the Postcard Printing Companies offer a neat swing ticket, which can include an image or logo for a reasonable price.

You must also remember to keep within the **Sales of Goods Act 1979** and be sure that the product for sale is fit for the purpose it was intended for e.g. if a piece of pottery is described as oven proof, it must be oven proof. Goods and their materials must not be mis-described. Another Act to be aware of is **The Consumer Protection Act 1987** which protects the public from death or injury, so all goods must be safe - i.e. toys with no sharp edges, glazes used on food containers (plates/bowls etc.) non toxic.

Plenty of further advice on 'Getting Paid' can be found in the previous article by Alison Branagan also on **www.**payontime.co.uk
which is another useful site, giving tips on how to avoid problems before they happen, adn how to get out of them if they have!

Copyright & Commissions

Furniture by Danielle and Selwyn Holmes, Dansel Gallery

With your name on a selection of registers and your photos possibly being seen by numerous different people and businesses, now is a good point to consider copyright issues. Ideas cannot be owned, unless they can be transferred onto paper which can then be owned by registering it as one of the following. They then become your legal property to sell, hire or rent out. The following brief descriptions are given by The Patent Office:

A Patent

Patents protect a new invention for what it is or does or how it works and is made.

To get a patent for an invention/design it must be new, no one else must know about it - so keep it quiet before applying. Patent protection can be given for up to 20 years with an annual fee. Anyone wishing to use your invention needs your permission and possibly will have to pay for the right.

A Copyright

Copyright protects drawings, text, songs, computer programmes anything artistic or aesthetic. It is free and automatic from the moment of creation, just put the copyright symbol, with name & date, on your work. Permission must be sought for anyone to copy this work.

A Design

A design can be registered to protect how something looks, but not how it works or what it does. e.g. a wallpaper pattern, the shape of a chair or pot. However the design must be individual and not resemble any existing designs. 12 months after disclosing the new design you must apply for a registered design. Protection starts from this date. The design can be registered for up to 25 years with fees due every five years.

Trade Marks

Trade Marks indicate who makes a product. Logos, signs, shapes, colours can all be registered as trade marks. Trade marks help people to recognise who made a product, they give confidence to the buyer. They can be registered forever with a fee due every ten years.

In the case of registers, each should deal with the copyright for their own database. Some will include a computer generated water mark on all images shown on the internet, to prevent them being printed and copied. Work displayed on the Internet is protected, in the UK, in a similar way to all other media. If you wish to download a piece of work you should check that permission is available first. Equally a piece of your work should not be copied from the Internet unless you have agreed in writing. However it is up to you to check on the arrangements made by each register or database to put

Copyright gives you, the creator, control over who has the right to copy your creative work.

your mind at rest.

As you can see in the front page of this book I have claimed the copyright for **Second Steps** and listed the forms of copying which are not permitted without my permission.

Claiming and enforcing copyright is surprisingly easy. It is automatic in the UK and, apparently, most of the world. It is a private right for the person concerned, they can therefore decide how to enforce copyright if or when necessary.

In the UK copyright protection is automatic with no registration or fees. It is not even necessary to mark the work with the international copyright mark, although some other countries do require this, followed by the name of the copyright owner and year of creation or publication. This seems a fairly simple and cheap way to stake your claim.

A member of my family, who did not do this, had a text copied after leaving it, as an example of his work, after an interview. Only to find it had been published some time later. Obviously it is easy for people to copy from a book like this. On one occasion, with one of the Craft Galleries Guides, it was brought to my attention that someone had photocopied pages and used them in

✳ It is essential to retain ownership of your original drawings, designs, models etc. which should be signed and dated as and when created.

an exhibition catalogue. This was an unimportant matter and a polite letter, pointing out the infringement, was all that was required to alert the person to their mistake and I received an apology.

However if the infringement involved copying a design and reusing it for financial benefit, this could be more serious and the injured party could consider taking advice from their local trading standards department or the police.

Whilst researching for the first edition of this book, I read many articles written by other people either for themselves or sometimes for particular publications. I wrote to a couple of groups whose work I was considering incorporating into the text of the book. One replied quickly with a form for me to sign, which clearly confirmed which parts I wished to use and for what purpose. In this way both parties were clear about what was being done and for what permission had been given, at no charge. Whereas another group, which involved several different writers wished to make a substantial charge to cover the cost of arranging agreements.

Freelance designers will own the copyright for their own designs; whilst designs created when at work are owned by the employer.

It is always wise to ask before copying, but as Copyright lasts until 70 years after the death of the author/creator where individually made, it may sometimes be difficult to track down the right person. In most cases the copyright owner will be co-operative. Copyright on the design of mass produced items only lasts for 25 years.

ACID, Anti Copying in Design
Adelaide House
London Bridge
EC4R 9HA
T: 0845 6443617
E: help@acid.uk.com
www.acid.uk.com
A trade association whose aims are to prevent copyright theft, by providing legal advice (incl 30 mins free) for each query. A logo is provided to be used on stationery and at exhibitions they also hold a register of new designs. Annual fees start at £95 + VAT

British Copyright Council
29-33 Berners Street
W1T 3AB
T: 01986 788 122
www.britishcopyright.org
National consultative and advisory body

DACS, Design and Artist's Copyright Society
33 Great Sutton Street
London
EC1V 0DX
T: 020 7336 8811
E: info@dacs.co.uk
www.dacs.org.uk
DACS is a copyright and collecting society for visual
artists. DACS issues licenses and collects revenue on
members behalf, and protects and promotes the
copyright of visual artists in the UK and worldwide.
Life membership £25+VAT

The Office of the Data Protection Registrar
Wycliffe House
Water Lane
Wilmslow
SK9 5AF
T: 01625 545745

Design Protect
Margaret Briffa
Business Design Centre
52 Upper Street
Islington
N1 0QH
T: 020 7288 6003
www.designprotect.com

Design Protect provides all the essential tools designers need to become aware of their rights and protect themselves. For an annual fee £40 + VAT
More information about insurance and legal problems:
www.briffa.com

Own It
University of the Arts London
The London College of Communication
Elephant and Castle
SE1 6SB
T: 020 7514 7985
E: info@own-it.org
www.own-it.org:
Your Free Intellectual Property Resource Centre
Own It is a new service which offers free intellectual property advice for London's creative people.

The Patent Office
Room 1L02
Concept House
Cardiff Road
Newport
NP10 8QQ
T: 0845 9500505
E: enquiries@patent.gov.uk
www.patent.gov.uk

Commissions

Now that you have details on several databases/registers and have decided on the best way to deal with your copyright, you are ready to receive a commission. There are several groups of people who may approach you concerning a commission:

Private

Many galleries offer a commissioning service to their buyers; serious collectors often think of this as their first choice and enjoy having something made just for them.

Public

Registers and Databases with groups and Regional Art Boards are more likely to be seen by professionals like architects/interior designers/councils and schools seeking artists for town or community projects or residencies. However the maker and the commissioner are introduced, the process and points to be considered are much the same.

Perhaps one of the most important and difficult aspects to learn is how to communicate your ideas.

- Use language that is not too technical,

- become a sensitive diplomat able to interpret your client's ideas in a realistic manner,

- be enthusiastic and encouraging so that they have confidence in your ability to work with them and create what they really want.

Commissions

Once satisfactory dialogue has been achieved is a good time to confirm what you have agreed on paper. ✳ **Always** make notes of all discussions and confirm every decision in writing, finally producing a contract for both parties to sign.

If you are providing sketch designs for them to take home, remember the cautionary tale from the copyright section and be sure that you have signed your sketch with your name and claimed the copyright, to prevent your client showing it to another designer and maybe asking for another (cheaper) price for your original piece of work.

As discussions progress, assuming this is a commission to make a one-off piece of work, the following points should be included on some form of document, of which both parties will have a copy :

- The names and contact addresses for both parties,

- The materials to be used for the work,

- The planned schedule for drawings and work,

- Delivery arrangements, allowing for extra people or expenses if a difficult piece to handle.

✳ Keep records of every conversation, phone call etc. related to your commission, it could be vital evidence to refer to if there is any difference of opinion later.

Commissions

- The cost and method of payment i.e. if part payment is required on acceptance of estimate, part mid-way and final on delivery.

- Who will own the copyright once the piece is sold.

- If the client decides not to go ahead, make clear if you will charge a design fee to cover your initial time spent in discussion and preparatory sketches.

- Insurance - make clear when your responsibility for this ends and when the new owner takes over.

- If the commissioning body gains publicity for your work they should credit you as the maker.

- If the work becomes damaged they should give you the first opportunity to carry out the repairs.

If your work is part of a residency check the contract carefully. It should include a clause for introducing an impartial arbitrator, should any unforeseen problems arise. If the commission is part of a residency, you may be invited to run workshops, lectures or other activities alongside the project. Your time allocated for these activities and relevant meetings must be paid for and therefore should be included in your estimates and in the final contract.

Commissions

Furniture by
Danielle & Selwyn
Holmes of
Dansel Gallery

Workshops for Designers

- Entrepreneurship
- Business Start-up
- Enterprise Skills
- Legal Issues
- Presentation
- Portfolio
- Self-Promotion

alison branagan

creative consultancy

Creative Industry Specialist

For information about workshops consultancy & enterprise support

visit www.alisonbranagan.com
contact alison@alisonbranagan.com
phone +44 (0) 20 8365 0453

Negotiation by Alison Branagan

Alison Branagan who runs her own business as a creative consultant, established courses and gives one to one advice. (See details on previous page). Alison has generously written the following piece about the art of negotiation; vital to achieve a successful commission.

Negotiation is the art of achieving your goals through discussion and bargaining. The best type of negotiation is a 'Win Win' scenario where both sides are happy with the outcome - which can be difficult!

We base our negotiations in business upon agreeing a deal; we may often require more money, time and/or resources, than initially is on offer. 'You don't get what you deserve, you get what you negotiate'. *Chester L. Karrass.* I used to think this was a rather trite quote, however over the years I have found it is the bold truth.

Designers often find talking about money awkward, when deciding what to charge for design services or for sales of their work. One has to toughen up a bit and recognise that earning a living from design means learning some business skills and becoming confident in discussions involving pricing and fees with the client. Learning as much as you can about industry or market rates is a necessity.

Focusing solely on getting the most money can sometimes be a 'red herring', by that I mean there are other factors that may be worth more than the actual

Negotiation by Alison Branagan

amount being offered. This is important to bear in mind when thinking through the negotiation process. Think carefully before you start negotiating; understand the mindset of the person or group of people you are talking to. ✳ What would you expect, require or try to achieve in their shoes?

In contract negotiations do not be fooled by encouraging emails about agreements for example, until you have the contract in your hands and you have studied it. With my work for various design organisations looking through contracts can be a mine-field, of 'rights grabs' (gaining ownership of your copyright) or other clauses that control or limit your rights as the creator.

The seven-step outline below is to help you think in a more business like way. During any discussion with clients or customers have some goals and also boundaries in mind. For example what is the best outcome you strive for, and what is the minimum offer you will accept?

✳ Alison suggests trying to see the situation from the other persons point of view - thinking what you might be asking for in their position.
This is a good tip- as this will keep you ahead of the game.

Negotiation by Alison Branagan

The seven key areas of negotiation:

1. Copyright and ownership

For designers/makers or illustrators the main issues are usually connected with copyright, design right and the licensing of products or surface designs/illustration for re-print, re-use, reproduction or merchandising in some form. In most cases it is down to you to either design your own contracts with an Intellectual Property Lawyer, or accept/negotiate contracts from the publisher, agent, retailer or manufacturer. Remember the basic elements of any licensing agreement are:

- duration,

- purpose,

- use and geographical location, e.g. UK wide, or worldwide.

2. Importance of time

This is often a very important issue in negotiation and is completely overlooked. Always ask for more time than is offered to you to create the commission or project. Why? Well for many reasons, the main two being

a) if you ask for more time, then that gives you time to take on other opportunities that arise and allows for any mistake or wastage of time.

b) Time for creative work can be difficult to estimate, especially if you are working with others, so best to build in flexibility.

Negotiation by Alison Branagan

3. Resources

Space, equipment, materials, advice, assistance, mailing lists, media exposure, etc. are examples of other elements in a negotiation process that can sometimes be worth more than the money involved in the initial project. If you are struggling with the negotiation process, i.e. you don't think you are getting paid enough, look through the project costs. If for example the cost of space is draining your budget then see if the client could offer space for a short time at no cost. Otherwise is there anything in kind that the client/business could offer you in return, in addition to the payment being offered?

4. Risk issues

This is my favourite, as it is an invisible danger, and difficult to spot. In any negotiation the client may off load as much risk as possible on to you. For example when you are running design/art workshops for an arts organisation or college the deal is often: that if the workshop is advertised, (e.g. in brochures or prospectus) and is then unfortunately cancelled or insufficient students enrol - you won't get paid. You still have to reserve this time out of your year, which you can't allocate to other opportunities. (You must value your time!) It's best not to commit yourself to a large number of workshops in the first year of working with an organisation, until the numbers build up.

Negotiation by Alison Branagan

5. Money and funding

Interestingly fees and payments are lower down on the list, because some of the other points can be more important in the longer term. Try to find ways of making more money from your work, creative services or sale of products/art pieces. Be prepared for buyers to offer less than the sales price, and devise a strategy for managing this situation. For example you are a furniture designer and you have made a large table, which is made of glass and fits together in sections. The client wishes to barter the price down. One idea would be to subtly make the purchaser realise that the price displayed 'could' include professional delivery and installation, (i.e. you in a van and wearing cotton gloves!). The cost to the client in money and time sourcing a suitable firm and paying for it (you will convey) far outweighs the asking price.

6. Goodwill

Again this is an almost invisible part in the negotiation process, I refer back to the 'Win Win' scenario. As soon as negotiations develop into a 'Win Lose' situation this is where the danger lies. When either party in negotiation feel that they are not getting what they ask for, the possibilities for future collaborations are reduced e.g. one party will look for someone else to work with, often unbeknown to the other, for future projects.

Negotiation by Alison Branagan

7. Credit and reputation

It is my belief that giving fair credit and an acknowledgement to creators or organisations who have assisted, advised, helped or sponsored you should be given wherever possible, either verbally or in printed credit. Also reputation is an important factor in your career. Association e.g. with reputable organisations or design agencies or companies, can aid you in gaining recognition within your chosen field. Make sure, if you are negotiating future use of images for example, that there is reference to yourself or your business name in its reproduction where possible. Failure to consider this aspect could harm your professional relationship e.g. 'loss of good will' as described above.

There are many other factors to discuss in negotiating skills such as how you build trust, presenting yourself and being confident.

Useful reading and organisations are:
The Association of Illustrators: **www**.theaoi.com
(Any publications by Simon Stern on 'Rights' or contracts via the AOI)
The Creators' Rights Alliance : **www**.creatorsrights.org
Any business publication on Negotiation Skills
Dorling Kindersley DK 'Negotiation Skills':
 www.dk.com DK Publishing produces a range of useful mini guides in practical enterprise skills.

Commissions - General notes

Whatever the commission, enjoy the experience and try to take as many photographs as possible, keep any press reports or other publicity for your portfolio/website; these can be used to impress future commissioners.

Several makers confirm the importance of the following points in their case studies:

4 P's PLANNING (research)

    PHOTOGRAPHS

    PERSEVERANCE (commitment)

    PATIENCE

- First stop for advice **www**.arts.org.uk

- Be realistic and do not under estimate money and time,

- Networking with other makers is helpful, consider joining a guild or society,

- Good communication skills are important,

- Be positive - enthusiastic - believe in your product,

- Be open to change and new ideas, think laterally.

It takes time to start a new business so be patient.

Matthew Burt Case study

In the 1970's **Matthew Burt** and his wife bought a rambling old house in the Wiltshire countryside. It was from here that he first began to make and sell furniture. Starting off with a few commissions, the business eventually grew into what it is today; a successful and professionally run organisation which has won many awards for its beautifully crafted and innovative designs. Still operating from the same house in Wiltshire, Matthew's wife acts as Principal Administrator while four assistants and one apprentice are employed in the busy workshop.

Having been in the craft business for many years Matthew has gained a vast range of experience and has plenty of good advice to offer. Due to the fact that every business rests upon this, he cannot emphasise enough the importance of perfecting ✳ the technique of presenting and communicating one's ideas:

> ✳ The importance of good communication skills are emphasised yet again.

Matthew Burt Case study

"I attempt to encourage people to spend, often sizeable amounts, just through my enthusiasm and on a two dimensional representation of an idea. I've yet to make it, neither of us has seen it. At present 80% of my work comes from me selling an idea, before it becomes an object. To do this requires the same degree of thought, passion, commitment and skill as the eventual making of the object".

When Matthew first set-up it was not unusual for him to visit a potential client in their own home, maybe two or three times to discuss a particular brief. Although a good way of securing work and forming relationships it did become expensive and time consuming. These days he will visit a client just once in the initial stages and thereafter, if the design process needs to be discussed further, will encourage them to visit him at his workshop.

"The relationship between the maker and client is at its best, almost symbiotic. We both have what the other wants. It's the same timeless exchange. Idea and object for cash or kind. After 25 years of designing and making my clients continually amaze me. Over the last few years the percentage of our work involving past clients is increasing. This makes logical sense and it must mean we're doing something right. Our response is to find imaginative means of keeping in contact with past clients. The main object is to ✳ treat each client with the same attention to detail so that their exchange with us

Matthew Burt Case study

is a success, sufficient for them to wish to return again".

Another area that Matthew places emphasis on is that of 'mentoring' and the need for craftspeople to communicate with one another. Most makers have had no formal business training and usually have to learn through trial and error. Also the nature of many crafts means the hours are often long and unsociable. The combination of the two can sometimes make for a lonely existence, especially through the difficult moments:

"The practice of designing and making is often solitary and isolating. Like many designer makers I'm incarcerated in a shed in the middle of nowhere with my work and I need to get out more! David Kay, the Crafts Officer with Southern and South Eastern Arts was ideally placed to haul me in from the seductive slide into defensive bigotry. He and his organisation acted as a mentor/catalyst between me and other individuals climbing the same hill. I was encouraged to meet and discuss with these fellow travellers, facing similar problems and at different stages upon that hill. I was able to take solace from, learn from and hold the hand of others".

※ Make your clients feel really special, give them your full attention and make life as easy as possible for them, so they remember the process of working with you as enjoyable.

Matthew Burt Case Study

Matthew would ideally like to see more organisations such as these in place. Due to a general lack of funding in the arts there is a distinct shortage of them. He points out, many businesses fail after three years and although this can be for a variety of reasons it is often due to a lack of guidance. It is therefore sometimes necessary for makers to set up co-operatives of their own. This is well worth doing if it helps to relieve the pressures and strains that new and old businesses present.

M.B.
www.matthewburt.com

Workshops

Workshops

Finding and funding a workshop

At some stage (probably quite early in your career) you will have to make the decision - whether to stay at home, where overheads are cheap but in most cases, space and freedom are limited, or to move into a rented workshop space.

Renting a small workshop is probably the ideal scenario to start off but this is not always easy to find. Alternatively sharing workshop accommodation is often a happy solution and gives you the support of other like minded people with similar problems with whom to communicate - rather than working in solitary silence.

Planning Permission

You would also be wise to check the terms of your lease/tenancy agreement/mortgage/existing house insurance to be sure that there is nothing in the small print preventing you from running a small business and that your stock and materials will be covered. It is much better to ask first before going to the expense of setting up only to find you are liable to be fined or refused permission for breaching the regulations. Ensure that 'permitted user' is being observed.

Business Rates/Council Tax

Another area to check is the rates/council tax. Business rates become due on any area of the home which is clearly used for business, on a permanent basis. If you use the dining room table for sewing up children's clothes, but only on a few evenings a week, council tax

Health & Safety

would remain as the only charge. However if one room or an outside shed was used permanently for throwing pots, this particular area would be charged at the business rate, whilst the rest of the home would remain on the council tax rate. It is advisable to seek **advice from your District Valuation Officer.**

If you are still keen to find a workshop to rent, you should first decide if it is to be used as a show room as well as a studio. If so the **location will be of prime importance.** You will need to do some serious market research to decide which areas will be best to attract your buyers.

Whereas if the space is to be a studio/workspace only, it really won't matter so much if it is on a prime trading route or not, as long as it is convenient for you. The search for a property will be an exciting and possibly frustrating challenge via:

- estate agents, local councils who may have a list of possible commercial buildings, local papers and your local Business Link

- Guilds are also a useful source of information about workshops

- If it is not essential for you to be in your immediate local area the national arts magazines sometimes advertise workshop spaces.

Health & Safety

Occasionally space is advertised in return for some work e.g. helping in a craft shop whilst using a workshop space.

'HSE Books' ✳ supply several free leaflets and booklets, you can contact them for a list of publications.
www.hse.gov.uk

This website has a useful drop down search list, once you select your subject - e.g. if working with chemicals check COSHH (Control of Substances Hazardous to Health) an informative page appears plus leaflets to print off. Many topics are covered including risk assessment and **first aid**. Even if you work on your own (and therefore have no responsibility for anyone else) it is a good idea to have some basic first aid knowledge. It would also be sensible to have emergency help numbers, clearly written, pinned up somewhere near you telephone. A basic first aid kit is also an essential piece of equipment.

A very important danger to consider is fire. A telephone call to your local fire station will put you in touch with their safety officer who will arrange to visit your premises and give you **free advice**.

Legal paperwork

✳ HSE hotline **T:** 0845 345 0055
www.hse.gov.uk
All books and leaflets can be ordered online.

Legal

LFYB is a scheme run by The Law Society to help small businesses get started. A number of offices throughout the UK participate. They offer a free half hour consultation and several step-by-step guides on business topics including: taking on leased business premises, structuring and raising money for your business and contracts with customers and suppliers.

If you are renting, buying or leasing it is sensible to seek the advice of a solicitor to deal with the legal paperwork. Whenever you are considering employing a professional adviser be sure to ask for a written estimate, to show how much they will charge for their services, before you instruct them to carry out any work. (These fees should be included in your business plan).

If you are renting, the landlord will usually expect the tenant to pay the costs of drawing up the lease. To reduce your expenses you can try at least to share these costs. This should be dealt with by your ✳ solicitor. Whether you are buying or leasing, it is advisable to have a structural survey of the property before making any decision. It is better to be warned of any serious defects before they happen and a leaky roof might change your mind about the property.

✳ Check fees before employing any professional.

Legal

Check what the adjoining buildings will be used for e.g. what will your neighbours be trading as - will they be compatible with your work?

Check with the Highways Dept. at your local Council Offices to see what is planned for the area in the long term e.g. if the area is to be pedestrianised for instance, which might make trading difficult, or maybe a supermarket is to be built nearby.

Check that there is sufficient parking space for you and your prospective customers in the vicinity.

If you are renting you must be confident that the terms of the lease are satisfactory for you, the tenant. The Landlord and Tenant Act 1954 gives security of tenure to business tenants, however this was amended in 1969. The landlord and tenant can now reach agreement excluding the tenancy from the 1954 Act, which means that you will have to vacate when your lease has expired. You will not have an automatic right to renew your lease at the end of the tenancy. You should also check to see who is responsible for the repairs to the building, both inside and out.

Law Society advice line T: 020 7405 9075
www.lawsociety.org.uk has a selection of leaflets on legal topics which you can download
www.solicitors-online.com
www.advice guide.org.uk the Citizens Advice line gives plenty of further guidance about Income Tax.

Legal

Another legal point which running a business raises is the need to make a Will. This is not something that many young people wish to think about, and being young and healthy it is highly unlikely it will be needed, but unfortunately accidents do happen. It is not expensive or difficult to make a will and if you have a successful business it would be wise to think how you would like it to continue or be divided. Also consider making an Enduring Power of Attorney, which will enable someone of your choice to deal with your affairs rather than the Court of Protection, should you become incapacitated for any reason.

Deposit

When you sign the contract, to buy, you are likely to be asked for a deposit. So now seems a good time to tackle the serious task of preparing a Business Plan, which will be an essential tool to take with you when applying for funding.

Income Tax & National Insurance

If you plan to be self employed you do need to consider your future, as no one else will. Although it is understandable that, if you are young, you cannot visualise ever needing a pension and suspect it is a waste of money, one day you will be glad that you bothered. You should contact your local DSS office and arrange direct debit payments for Class two NI contributions, at present approx £3 per week. If these are missed you may have to pay extra.

Partnerships

If you make a profit of over £4,895 you will have to pay 7% on the surplus. It is recommended that you put aside 15% of your profits to cover these expenses

Although, at this stage, it is unlikely that you will have any spare cash, you should be aware of the benefits of saving a little on a regular basis. Mini ISA's are a good way to save small amounts and save paying Tax. Contact your local ✳ tax office who can provide many free leaflets. There is also plenty of advice on setting up your own business on the Dept.for Work & Pensions. **www.dwp.gov.uk/resource centre**

A Sole Trader is self explanatory. Yours will be the only signature on all cheques, you will be the only person responsible for your business - if all goes well you will take all the profit, if not you will bear all the losses. Profits drawn or not are taxed as profit. Losses can usually be offset against tax on other income.

A Partnership can consist of two or more people, who are working together for a common aim. You would need a legal partnership agreement to set out the rights and obligations of the partners.

An equity partner is someone putting in capital but this amount can vary between the partners, they can

✳ A newly self-employed person must register with the Inland Revenue as soon as they start work. A delay of three months, after starting work, and you could be penalised.

Companies

then take a proportional share of the profits. They all share responsibility for debts/losses.

A salaried partner means that you are not putting in any capital and therefore are not responsible for any debts but will receive a regular, guaranteed salary. You will still take an active role in the business. A partnership is dissolved if one of the partners dies, resigns or becomes bankrupt.

Limited Liability Partnerships were introduced in July 2001. Partners are taxed as individuals but have to file their accounts at Companies House - only relevant to large businesses.

A Limited Liability Company

A Company is governed by the Companies Acts, which means that accounts must be audited each year, an annual fee paid to Companies House and a copy of the accounts filed with Companies House.(Except in the case of small companies). The owners of the Company are called Directors if they go bust their liability is usually limited to up to £10 each. You need to check the Memorandum and Articles of Association.

If a company is successful and wishes to expand it can sell shares to raise capital. Dividends may be paid to shareholders. A company has 'perpetual existence' as it is regarded as a separate entity from the owners.

A valuable site to keep if you are planning to set up on your own. **www.dwp.gov.uk/resource centre**

Business Name

Business Name

If you form a Limited Company you can obtain a booklet from Companies House giving advice or check their website. Restrictions on names and on what information you must give are the same whatever type of business you are running.

If you trade under a name other than your own there are special regulations to be met.
www.companieshouse.gov.uk and

National Business Register Plc

Somerset House
40-49 Price Street
Birmingham
B4 6LZ
T: 0121 678 9000
E: sales@start.biz
www.start.biz

British Council Arts Group
www.britishcouncil.org/arts

Department of Trade Industry & the Regions

Enquiries: **T:** 020 7215 5000
www.dti.gov.uk
This website has links to Companies House, Business Link and many other useful sites.

Business Advice

Below are a few useful contacts for business advice
Business Link Offices
National Contact **T:** 0845 600 9006
www.businesslink.org
who will put you in touch with your local office.

Chambers of Commerce
www.britishchambers.org.uk
Offices throughout the country will give advice on
business related topics.

Clerkenwell Green Association
Pennybank Chambers
33 -35 St. John's Square
London
EC1M 4DS
T: 020 7251 0276
E: info@cga.org.uk
www.cga.org.uk
A central London organisation with 80 workshops in
their complex and many schemes to help new makers
start up workshops and businesses.

Workshops/Support

Cockpit Arts
Cockpit Yard,
Northington Street
London
WC1N 2NP
T: 020 7419 1959
E: info@cockpitarts.com
www.cockpitarts.com
Cockpit Arts provides start-up facilities/opportunities
for approximately 100 designer-makers. Studio space
is available through the Seedbed Award Scheme.

Design Trust
41 Commercial Road
E1 1LA
T: 020 7320 2895
E: petalevi@designnation.co.uk
www.designnation.co.uk
Promotes young designers through its catalogue and
website but also provides business guidance. Publishes
Business Start-up a Guide for Designers and Makers.

Workshops/Support

Hidden Art
Shoreditch Stables
Ground Floor Rear
138 Kingsland Road
London
E2 8DY
T: 030 7729 3800
E: info@hiddenart.co.uk
www.hiddenart.com
Designer makers in UK may join for membership £25,
although they specialise in promoting London makers.

Ideas Factory
www.ideasfactory.com
Plenty of advice on setting up a business particularly for
creative people.

Mazorca Projects Ltd.
Shoreditch Stables
Ground Floor Rear
138 Kingsland Road
London
E2 8DY
T:020 7729 3800
E:info@ hidden art.co.uk
www.hiddenart.com
Supports long term development of creative businesses
in Hackney.

Insurance

Gareth Huxtable Dip CII from TH March gives some general advice on insurance topics

Congratulations! You have successfully completed your studies and have decided to apply your skills and knowledge to run your own craft business. You have probably already formulated a business plan, researched your markets, found suitable premises and are ready to start trading; but have you considered what insurance protection you need?

Getting Started

When starting up in business budgets can be tight, and insurance is often seen as a luxury to be done without. However, nothing could be further from the truth. Any business whether large or small faces uncertainty and risk and is particularly vulnerable during its infancy, where even a small unwelcome incident can have a disastrous effect on the success of the enterprise. Insurance is ignored at one's peril and should be viewed as an essential requirement in order to protect the assets, earnings and liabilities of the business. It could also be the case that insurance cover has to be arranged either by law or as a requirement to obtaining a loan, grant or lease or to be allowed to attend a trade fair or exhibition. How does one go about deciding what insurance is needed? As already mentioned the areas which need protection are the assets, earnings and liabilities of the business.

Insurance

Liabilities at Law

Probably the most important aspect, which should be given priority, is to arrange liability cover to provide protection against legal liabilities incurred to pay damages and legal costs due to negligence, arising during the course of trading. In both our personal and business lives we all owe a duty of care to others which arises under both Common Law and Statute. If we fail in that duty of care we can be held liable to pay damages for any harm caused such as injury to a third party or damage to their property.

Public and Products Liability insurance should be arranged in this respect with a limit of indemnity probably not less than £2,000,000 to reflect that court awards and legal costs continue to rise and the fact that we all live in an increasingly litigious society. Typical examples of claims which can arise under this class of insurance include where members of the public visit your workshop or studio and trip or fall over a hazard or where a product you make causes injury.

Employees

In addition, if you employ any persons (even part-time or only for a short period) you must arrange Employers Liability insurance by law, which provides protection in the event of the employee being killed or injured due to your negligence whilst working for you.

Insurance

Assets

The assets of the business relate to the actual property which is owned or for which the business is responsible. The assets usually relate to such items as machinery, tools, trade contents, stock, materials in trade, money and buildings. Insurance cover can be arranged on such assets either for specified events e.g. loss or damage caused by fire or theft or on an 'All Risks' basis. Care needs to be exercised to always ensure that the sums to be insured always represent the full value at risk. The cover arranged should not only operate at your own premises but should also be capable of being easily extended to provide cover elsewhere e.g. whilst in transit or whilst at other locations such as exhibitions and galleries.

Income Protection

With regard to protecting the earnings (income) of the business there are two aspects of insurance cover to which thought needs to be given. Firstly, if your premises are destroyed or damaged you might not be able to trade fully for a period, which could result in loss of earnings. Protection against such an eventuality can be insured under a form of insurance called Business Interruption. The second aspect, which could affect your earnings, is if you are unable to trade due to either illness or injury and some form of Personal Income Protection policy may be necessary. There are many

Insurance

types available ranging from low cost Personal Accident covers to policies which provide protection over long periods due to serious disability or sickness.

The above is only an outline of the critical areas of insurance that any business needs to consider. As your business grows and develops other types of insurance may also become necessary which may include Legal Expenses, Critical Illness, Life Insurance and Pension arrangements.

Relevant points which you will need to watch for when initially buying insurance cover are :

1. If you operate from your home you must tell your household insurer what you are doing. It is unlikely that your household policy will automatically include your business activities.

2. If you use your own car for business use you must declare the fact to the insurers concerned.

3. Never assume that if you entrust your goods to someone else e.g. a gallery, that their insurance automatically insures your goods. Always double check the position.

4. Never assume your own policy automatically covers your goods away from you own premises. Read your policy wording carefully and, if necessary, arrange appropriate extensions.

Insurance

How to arrange cover

So, you are about to start trading and have a basic idea of what insurance protection you wish to purchase but how do you go about arranging such cover at the right price?

As with buying any product or service it will pay to shop around and it will almost certainly be in your best interests to engage the services of a specialist insurance broker who will be able to provide you with professional and independent advice at no direct cost. Insurance brokers are authorised and regulated by the Financial Services Authority and have to comply with various conditions regarding solvency, accounting practices and professional indemnity cover. They must always act in the best interests of their client and will often assist in the settlement of claims on behalf of their client.

Gareth Huxtable Dip CII is an Associate Director of T.H. March & Co.Ltd., Insurance Brokers who have been established for over 100 years and specialise in arranging insurances for the Craft, Jewellery and Giftware trades.

Galleries

Ceramics by Julian Belmonte

Galleries - overview

The following section deals with selling through galleries, which has been one of the most popular methods for years. However the growth of technology may be forcing us to reconsider the best way to sell contemporary crafts in the 21st Century. Having run my own Galleries for ten years I am well aware (from both sides) of some of the problems which may occur. Even so, while researching for this section, I have been surprised at the strength of feeling revealed by both gallery owners and exhibiting makers.

 A few makers started selling their work through the internet about eight years ago but now nearly every maker has their own site, so it has become common practice. As you will read in the following pages, highlighting the views of two gallery owners, this causes serious problems for them. However speaking to some of the makers, particularly those selling larger items, difficult to display in a gallery setting, I have heard a strong defence for internet and craft show sales.

 I realise that both sides must be considered carefully if new ways of dealing with sales to the public are to be evolved; there are many pros and cons for galleries, internet and show to be considered.

The fully illustrated Craft Galleries Guide, published bi-annually by BCF Books, is another good way to research suitable galleries to stock your work. www.bcfbooks.co.uk

Galleries - overview

One maker pointed out that without makers the galleries would not exist, of course this is true. However Dillon Rudge and Julian Belmonte (pages 182 & 186) both sing the praises of galleries, explaining how the support of a good gallery enables them to concentrate on making. They have realised that working with the gallery owner to build a good relationship benefits them both. This is the secret-communicate with your gallery right from the start and clear any issues about prices which may arise.

Several professional makers who I have spoken to have resolved the problem by creating very good web sites to promote their own work, then listing all their outlets, with links. This way both parties benefit, the galleries get extra visitors via the particular maker's site and hopefully the maker gains extra sales which he/she has not had to waste time over (beyond the web site).

The decision to use galleries, or craft shows and/or the internet is a personal choice but remember to think the whole process through before making a decision.

If you decide that galleries could help you find a market, I hope that the following case studies will be helpful to you. Not only in considering the best way to approach a gallery and understand exactly what service that gallery should be offering you, but also how you should respect and work with a gallery.

N.B. There are also section about selling via the internet on page 233 and craft shows page 203

Galleries - owners' view

Recently I have had conversations with two gallery owners who share a concern over the effect that maker's websites have on their gallery's turnover. Danielle Holmes and her husband Selwyn have been running Dansel Gallery, in Dorset for 26 years. Being furniture makers they started by stocking their own work alongside a few other wood workers. Over the years they have expanded to stock the work of 200 British makers, although 25% is still work designed by the owners. This makes their gallery one of only a handful who specialise entirely in wood.

While Sandra Bosanquet has only been running her jewellery gallery Bosanquet in Wales for four years. In 2005 she felt forced (by economic reality) to open a second, more commercial gallery selling British and some foreign work, in a prime site which she hopes will provide a good steady turnover, allowing her to specialise in designer jewellery in her first gallery.

Recently Danielle and Sandra have suspected that gallery sales have suffered because many of their makers have their own websites. Customers, after visiting a gallery to view and learn more about the work now expect to find a maker and their sales site by just popping their name into Google search. Sales can then be made directly from the maker's site, with no commission going to the gallery.

※ A maker needs a gallery as a writer needs an editor.

Bosanquet Contemporary Jewellery Galleries 1 & 2
Haverfordwest & Pembroke Dock
T: 01437 769178

Dansel Gallery, Abbotsbury, Dorset
T: 01305 871515 **E**: danielle@danselgallery.co.uk
www.danselgallery.co.uk

Galleries - owners' view

New makers may well ask "Why not, we have to try every way possible to sell our work?" Of course this is true but equally the galleries have to make a living if they are to remain in business. The next question may be "Why do we need galleries?" In my opinion galleries take the same role for a ✳ professional maker as an editor does for a writer and are an essential part of the whole professional package. Perhaps **'professional'** is the key word here.

3D work needs to be seen in the round, to be touched and picked up. Displayed in the quiet, calm atmosphere of a gallery where the right ambience for buying quality work has been established, with expert staff on hand to answer any queries. A good gallery will work hard to promote their makers work, deal with the public and sales. In this way the maker is protected, whilst also being marketed and is able to give full attention to the task of actually designing and making.

When you read the Pricing section you will see how you are advised to consider carefully how much time you can actually give to making, pointing out that a great deal of time will be spent on administration etc. Therefore, although you may think that paying

✳ 'Buying time to make, by using a gallery to promote your work' maybe you can include the cost of commission in your pricing figures, so that it is covered in advance.

Galleries - owners' view

commission to a gallery is a waste of money, in fact you are ✳ buying more time to be creative and this may even allow you to earn more in the long run.

Danielle and Sandra's concern with internet selling is that makers will often undercut the price that a piece of work is sold at in the gallery, because the maker does not have the same overheads. (This used to be the problem with maker's workshop sales, when near to a host gallery, but that was just a local issue not national as today). There should be a good relationship between maker and gallery owner so that these issues can be discussed at the outset and retail prices agreed. Sandra was impressed by a quote from one of her suppliers who referred to ✳ 'Business Morality'. By this she meant that each should respect each other and the makers should certainly not undercut the gallery who is trying hard to work on their behalf.

However Sandra feels so strongly about this that she does not take on makers who plan to sell their work through direct selling events and the internet, as she says *"They should avoid the Farmer's Market mentality, selling produce direct to the public at wholesale prices and eliminating themselves from the commercial markets. They are in effect, setting themselves up to rely upon subsidy and handouts'*.

✳ Business Morality is mentioned a number of times as it is very important for gallery owners and makers

Galleries – owners' view

Danielle is always on the look out for new makers and is happy to be approached by them in a business like manner. e.g. Write first with a letter, CV and small selection of images, just to give an idea what you do. Follow up with a telephone call to see if the gallery is interested and arrange a time to show your work.

Danielle sometimes finds that a certain aspect of the work will let it down. If this is an area which can be improved (a plinth or the finish on the wood) she will ✳ give advice and if the maker follows this up she is quite happy to see the improved version at a later date. Gallery owners know what sells and how to display work, it is well worth listening to them and taking their advice, not getting upset and ignoring what they have said. If rejected at first, be positive and try again. (see p304)

Sandra has a great deal of experience with new makers having worked for a number of years at the Arts Council of Wales she recommends that makers should always follow up contacts made with gallery owners, at shows or over the telephone. Always remember to do what you say - sending samples, images whatever or if you are unable to follow up write to apologise.

If a gallery orders work at a show be sure that the work they receive is what they ordered i.e. don't' try

---

✳ Take advice with a good grace - it really can be helpful.

Galleries - owners' view

to fob them off with some older/different stock, because you are running short of time to make the repeat new work.

If a gallery pays by pro-forma invoice i.e. paying in advance, stick to the delivery date. Sandra remembers an instance when she had to wait three months after paying in advance - she obviously didn't order from that maker again. She has also had bad experiences with jewellers who have not supplied hall-marked work and then refused to take it back, a bad case of no 'Business Morality'.

Gina Frost who sells work to Bosanquet Gallery and first used the 'Business Morality' term has also given a few thoughts about dealing with galleries. Gina is a jewellery designer who now sells work for German designers to British galleries. She therefore has much experience dealing with galleries but from a slightly different angle.

Gina advises makers who are approaching galleries to create their own checklist and to research the gallery well before even considering applying. ✳ SOR can be mutually beneficial but both parties should be clear on their areas of responsibility so neither party is taken advantage of. Some (very few) galleries, who may be full of loud talk and enthusiasm to start with, are often

✳ Seller beware! Business Morality must work both ways.

keen to encourage makers to leave work on SOR, but once they have the work they do nothing more to promote that maker.

This is a dangerous situation for the maker; work may be tied up on SOR indefinitely, with little hope of actually selling and due to lack of professional marketing will not even be acting as an advertisement for the maker.※ When passing work on to a gallery on SOR it is important to clarify the terms. For instance who is responsible for damage? You must make clear that the goods must be returned in a saleable condition, if not the gallery is responsible and must pay you for them.

Negotiation is important to be sure that the gallery will provide the service that you expect and equally that you will work with the gallery as they require, and keep to any deadlines that are set.

As a new maker it is difficult to be self disciplined and take responsibility for yourself-you have to try and set yourself realistic deadlines and work hard to keep to them - think ahead. Do not take on too much too soon, and always be sure that you can meet orders, don't' just say yes and then wonder how to get the work done.

※ SOR can be dangerous - every so often a story like the one on page 180 about disappearing galleries, does the rounds and sends shivers down my back!

Approaching galleries

The following list was compiled by jeweller and one time gallery owner Clare John

- The first step is to research the gallery.

- Try and find out whether your work will fit into the gallery ethos.

- Look at magazines (e.g. Crafts and A-N) adverts, talk to people, read the Craft Galleries Guide or make a preliminary visit.

- Make a phone call. Be sure that you are speaking to the right person and introduce yourself.

- You can offer to send slides or photographs.

- Make an appointment to bring your work in.

Sometimes, if you know that the gallery is reputable (and not likely to disappear overnight, which happened to Clare once) it can be an idea to send a sample of your work. This is particularly useful when long distances are involved. If you make an appointment:

- Keep it and be punctual.

- Obviously you will dress smartly and tidily but it doesn't have to be in a conventional "suit" (you are an artist after all).

Approaching galleries

- Don't let yourself down by sloppiness.

- Present your work in a professional manner.

- Present well displayed and labelled.

- Know your work; the prices, materials, delivery times etc. It is a good idea to have a catalogue and C.V. whether it is photo-copied or printed on a computer, with at least one photograph, to leave as a reminder.

- Don't forget that a gallery owner's top priority is to the customer.

- Be prepared to wait if a customer needs serving, either while you are on the phone or visiting.

- Don't take up too much of the owner's time.

- If you say you will do something e.g. mail a catalogue, remember to do it.

Please don't be despondent if you are unsuccessful.
I know it's hard to walk away from being turned down and to feel positive. If you can, find out why your work is not right. Ask the gallery owner for advice, most will be happy to help.   C.J.

Dillon Rudge Case study

Dillon Rudge is a sculptural ceramicist and works from his home workshop on the outskirts of Bude, North Cornwall. Coming from a family of ceramicists, he studied this craft at 'Bristol Polytechnic of Art & Design', after which he gained further experience working with his father, Lawson Rudge Senior.

Dillon set up on his own about eight years ago producing Raku fired ceramic pieces. Most of his work focuses on animals, mainly influenced by the countryside he grew up in: 'Having lived in the countryside all my life, I have always been aware of various animals, both domestic and wild. Having explored all the different mediums in art I found clay modelling the most satisfying and rewarding. I therefore decided that combining clay with animal form was definitely the direction in which I was going.'

At first Dillon sold his work through a few galleries on a SOR basis. He was fortunate as he was able to use his father's equipment and workshop, avoiding the initial costs that can often cripple a new business. Dillon revealed that actually establishing himself was a 'slow process that very much relied upon making the right piece at the right time'. Over the years he has

Dillon Rudge Case study

discovered that there are definite trends in animal forms. He suggests keeping an eye on these by regularly visiting galleries, to see what is selling. More recently he has noticed an increase in demand for his barn owl sculptures, due to the popularity of 'Harry Potter' and his owl 'Hedwig'. As Dillon pointed out, 'I sculpted owls originally because they would swoop in front of me like a huge, white ghost when I was driving at night; I almost knocked the things over!'

Dillon is now affiliated to around 20 galleries, mainly in the South-West of England. Due to the delicate nature of his pieces he does not encourage studio visits. ✳ **He therefore finds galleries to be of particular use for their sympathetic display of his pieces, which allows the public to look closely, without fear of damage.** In addition to this, gallery employees have the

✳ Dillon obviously appreciates the benefit of the gallery space to show off his work, and highlights the possible dangers of visitors in a workshop.

Dillon Rudge Case study

knowledge to explain in detail how a certain piece has been made. Dillon considers this to be of great importance because the technique he uses is unique to him and can often be a good selling point.

Since being in business Dillon has also had a couple of bad experiences, one of which was with a gallery in London. The owner closed the gallery down and sold it to a new owner without informing him. When Dillon telephoned the gallery, on the off-chance, to enquire how his work was selling, he was not only surprised to find himself talking to a completely different owner but also to learn that the work he was enquiring about had been sold and he had apparently received payment! He had no record of this and had certainly not been paid but unfortunately could not prove it. He therefore strongly advises makers to ✳ '**keep in regular contact with galleries, and always keep alert to changes of ownership and keep a tally of your work!**'

Generally Dillon has a good relationship with galleries. Due to the rapid growth of the Internet most of galleries now have their own website, which in terms of promotion has proved to be invaluable to many craftspeople. As a result Dillon sells his work both nationally and internationally, particularly in the USA.

✳ Once again the problem of SOR is mentioned - so do take care when dealing with this method of payment.

Dillon Rudge sculptural raku ceramics

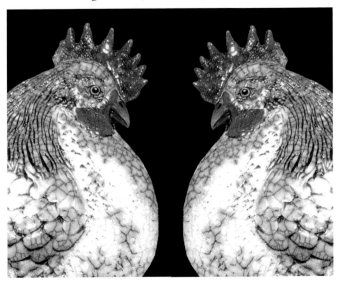

Julian Belmonte ceramics

Julian Belmonte Case study

Julian Belmonte Ceramics
www.julianbelmonte.co.uk

At college we were always told that when we leave we must strive for a studio to make our work in and find a string of galleries to sell it from. This sounds a simple formula, that should lead to a successful ceramic career. In practice however this can be a complex minefield that makers of all disciplines have to navigate.

Researching and approaching galleries with your work can be an exciting yet daunting experience, especially when it is time to discuss your prices and the gallery commission.

Gallery commission can be anywhere between 50-100% so think about the figure you would accept after the gallery has taken its commission before pricing your

Julian Belmonte Case study

work and keep it consistent through all your galleries.

As a result of forming close professional relationships with galleries, I have learned how much work is done on my behalf. In most cases we, as makers, are not as good as we may think we are at promoting ourselves and our work to others. However, this is a role that most galleries do well at. I have found that developing relationships with one or two galleries over a period of time can be very beneficial. As they gain confidence in your work, see its development, and sell it you are increasingly likely to have your work as their stock items, be involved in group exhibitions and eventually have a solo exhibition.

The commercial gallery can help raise your profile. It is often the case that a specialist periodical or lifestyle magazine will approach a gallery for features and information and on a particular type of work, so make sure the galleries have the best images of your work and a good work statement.

Above all, a relationship with a gallery should be seen as a partnership. Never be afraid to ask a gallery for help with your professional development.

J.B.

Like Dillon Julian realises how important galleries are to him and recognises the amount of work they do. As pointed out earlier there are a few exceptions to this good practice, so do check them out first.

Setting up a gallery

Many prospective gallery owners have contacted me over the past 16 years. Presumably hoping that my experience with the Craft Galleries Guide will have provided me with the blueprint for setting up a gallery-I wish that was so!

I have had a number of long telephone conversations with **enthusiastic** people wanting to run with their dreams and set up the perfect gallery. A handful of those people are still running galleries, a couple very successfully but sadly they are the exception.

❋ To make a living from running a gallery is very hard nowadays; if you can set up a gallery in the building where you live you obviously have a head start, with no rent to pay. Realistically most people have to go out and find a property, rent/buy it and often pay staff to help run the gallery once it is open.

There are no rules for setting up a gallery. The concept of your particular gallery must be original, with some new angle/idea which can become your USP. The business issues are the same as for any business so many sections in this book can be used as a guide. Market research and the actual position for your venue are more crucial than ever for a gallery business. I have been asked to address the following questions in particular:

❋ Be realistic and enthusiastic!

Setting up a gallery

Q1 How to contact makers

Q2 Is it better to invite well established makers or find new up and coming ones

A It would be wise to decide **2** first - in my view a mix of both would be best. The well known names are always good to have as it reassures some buyers to see names they know in your lists and attracts attention. Whereas others will be keen to discover new young makers. If you are lucky enough to find a new name, who is really good, this may help you with your USP, if you can persuade them to stay mainly with your gallery.

Q3 Which craft fairs to go to to find makers?

A 1 & 2: the list of shows (pages 222) is as useful for buyers as sellers but as to the best, I would recommend the New Designers Show as one of the best sources and websites like www.designtrust com and of course the Second Steps Portfolio section of **www**.bcfbooks.co.uk

Q4 How to price work realistically?

Q5 Is there a standard % to add on?

A 4 & 5: See the pricing section, there is no rule, if selling in London it will be a higher % ,as overheads are greater than in the country - many issues have to be taken into account. One of the main things is to fix selling prices with the maker so that they do not undercut you later.

Setting up a gallery

A 6   Research is the main thing here, see how your competitors display their work and decide what you admire most. The Crafts Council used to have a list of requirements for displays, when they still ran the Selected Galleries list. One was that there should be clear information about each maker, alongside their work. The style in which you choose to create displays is such a personal matter again there can be no rules. I enjoy simple uncluttered displays where it is possible to see each piece easily, without having to search amongst shelves of indifferent work.

Q7   Ideas for marketing the gallery

Q8   How to build a responsible relationship with the makers and gain their trust

Q9   SOR versus buying in work

A 7,8 & 9

These are all covered in Marketing & Galleries

Q10   Are Private Views useful?

A 10   As a gallery owner I often wondered, as my guests sipped their mulled wine and ate their mince pies. However on a more serious level if you can afford it I think the goodwill built up does pay off over time. Successful galleries will often sell much of the work prior to the PV, from the mini catalogue sent as an invitation or through their website.

Setting up a gallery

Although it can be depressing to spend a PV chatting to your artist/maker apologising for the lack of people/sales, nothing is better than the satisfaction when counting the red dots at the end of a successful Private View.

Finally, the original questioner said she had spoken to a number of established gallery owners. She reported that although many moaned about their insecure financial situation, they all clearly valued their work and wanted to share their enthusiasm for crafts with others. Without a passion for crafts there is no point in even thinking about opening a gallery.

Alpha Gallery, East Coker the first gallery I set up in converted stables in 1984.

Gallery owning maker

John McKellar Gallery owner & jeweller in Hereford,
highlights the pros and cons of running your own gallery

Pros :

- Selling at retail price maximises margin and profit
- Feed back from customers is very useful and can be confidence building too
- Higher perceived public profile
- Working in isolation in workshop/studio can be lonely
- Can add variety to working routine
- Can bring in one-off/commissions as well as selling stock

Cons:

- Running a retail outlet can be time consuming
- May make it difficult to design and produce, as interruptions can destroy concentration
- May involve commitment, being there full time

Gallery owning maker

- May bring high overheads and possibly capital investment
- Members of the public can be difficult/irritating
- Security problems more likely

Some makers run retail outlets and continue to make with great success, but many find that as the retail becomes established it becomes difficult to find the time or mental space to create.

This may be eased if more than one maker shares responsibility or if profits will support staff (but that can bring its own problems......).

J.M.

Gallery owning maker

As a maker you will almost certainly take part in an exhibition from time to time or even set up your own. As a gallery owner and an art centre administrator, (both at the same time for a few years), I found myself constantly looking ahead to deadlines and trying to remember to advertise the relevant shows. Planning is definitely a very important tool here.

If you run your own retail outlet, particularly if it is run on the lines of a gallery rather than a shop, you may find as I did, that you need to hold regular exhibitions to encourage repeat visits.

There are only so many times that one visitor will return to your venue each year, they really won't need a piece of jewellery every month or a new ceramic salad bowl more than once or twice in a lifetime.

Admittedly many people return to buy presents throughout the year but to give them an incentive it is useful to hold regular exhibitions. Christmas is obviously a good time to encourage present buying, but remember to set the date well ahead of the 25th, so that your visitors have time to search for presents and post them. List the tasks which need to be dealt with, plus dates when they should be done by. Try to give yourself plenty of time to plan an exhibition - at least six months.

The Venue :

- Is it suitable for an exhibition?
- If it is your gallery/shop there should be no

Running an exhibition

problems. However if it is the first time that you have used it for this purpose ask yourself the following questions:

- Is there enough space, if a large number of visitors arrive at one time?

- Where will they all park their cars?

- If it is raining where will umbrellas drip?

- If on the first floor, will the floor be strong enough to cope with an influx of people?

If you do not have your own gallery space you may have to use another venue. This might be a village hall, an empty shop window, a theatre foyer, a restaurant/cafe, a hired space in an Arts Centre or gallery, a library - whatever it is there will be different problems.

- How can the exhibition be displayed?
- Who will steward it?
- Is security covered day and night?
- Is insurance covered?

Consider the best time to put on your exhibition - for instance you will not want your event to clash with another local activity, or with any National Sporting event, annual holidays etc. With the venue and date

Running an exhibition

decided upon, the following points will be much the same wherever it is to be.

- Be sure that you have prepared display materials in good time.

- Will these be wooden painted plinths, glass display cabinets, purpose made units with locks, wooden planks on bricks.

There are numerous different ways to display work without being too contrived or extreme. The display or framing materials should never become more important than the work.

To acquire new ideas try to think laterally. As you walk around your high street, look at window displays and consider how you could use some of the ideas or items for sale. For instance plastic kitchen accessories can have many display uses. Discarded or out of date shop fittings or window display materials can often be acquired very cheaply and given a new life as your display background.

When you are arranging your exhibition space try to cut out all confusing clutter from the background (rather like composing a photograph). If there is a window with an ugly or distracting view you could hang translucent material or paper over it.

At one exhibition I was impressed by a room divider, created to shut off a workshop and provide display space. The makers had formed recessed shelves within the temporary timber wall. These were purpose made

Running an exhibition

Ted Franklin

for the items to be displayed, the whole unit was painted white with effective lighting pin pointing the work - simple but professional. (see above)

With the venue and date decided you will need to consider your publicity and whether you will have a Private View. Having made these decisions you will be able to cost the exhibition in detail and check that you are keeping within your budget, if not, now is the time to make adjustments. Try to think of all possible expenses, not just the obvious - will there be extra transport costs to deliver work, extra staff to employ for help?

Allow a contingency figure of say 10% of your total to cover anything you may have forgotten.

A Private View is always a good way to encourage

Running an exhibition

viewers, especially if you can afford to give them at least one free glass of wine. SOR wine is usually available from local shops who will also hire/loan you a box of glasses. If you can create a few interesting nibbles or (at Christmas) provide hot mince pies these will prove an added attraction. People certainly do enjoy a themed event, which can be very simple to organise.

Assuming that you are having a Private View you will need to prepare your invitations in good time, so that they can be sent out about two weeks before the event. The exact timing is up to you but too early and the invitations will be forgotten and if too late the guests may have previous engagements. The invitations themselves could be printed on the back of postcards which you already have, or specially prepared for the event. If you are ordering from Abacus, for instance, it is possible to have a certain number printed with the PV details and the remainder left blank.

However if funds are very low you can create hand made cards, which might be a work of art in themselves and could be an attractive feature as a free memento.

Hopefully you will have built up a mailing list by having a visitors book in your gallery/workshop and keeping a note of everyone who has bought work in the past.

You can also dredge through your address books for old contacts who might be interested to see what you are doing, besides sending to local dignitaries, funders,

Running an exhibition

RAB officers, gallery owners and anyone who you think might be keen to buy either now or in the future.

If you are running a mixed exhibition, with work by other makers you will obviously benefit from their mailing lists and must remember to print sufficient for them to have a bundle to send out as well. If you can afford to print a larger run than needed for the mailout, it can be useful (after seeking permission) to put small piles on the desks at hotels, arts centres, galleries etc. You will have given thought to your market and this will help you decide where will be the most useful place to direct your publicity.

At the same time as designing your PV cards you will probably decide to design a poster. Posters act as a useful reminder to come and visit your event. It is best to restrict them to A4 as space will be at a premium, in shops or wherever you wish to put them.

Unfortunately this all takes time, distribution in particular. However, it is worth building up contacts who will display your publicity, local shops and PO's, art shops, galleries, book shops, notice boards. TIC's and libraries are useful, if you can find their head office they may be willing to take several posters, for internal delivery to their 'regional clusters'.

If you prepare a Press Release and include some photographs you may be successful in gaining free editorial in your local papers. You may even persuade their photographer to come and record the exhibition.

Running an exhibition

As the date for your exhibition draws near check back through your list of tasks. Make sure you have asked any extra helpers to keep the evening free and that you have put aside time for the actual setting up. If you wish to have flowers or Christmas greenery check that you have time to collect and arrange them.Remember to leave time for numbering the work exhibited and preparing the catalogue. Even if this is a simple list with just the numbers, titles and prices it will still take time at the last minute and then need to be copied.

Finally stock up on red stickers to identify all the items sold and check that you have a receipt book. Then sit back and enjoy the event, communicating with your potential future customers.

There is plenty more detailed information about preparing a ✳ Press Release on page 77.

✳ www.startups.co.uk/Pressandnbsp_ releases

To find lists of Craft Galleries:
Craft Galleries Guide -by BCF Books
Crafts Magazine
www.goodgalleryguide.com/
www.icga.co.uk

Direct Selling via Craft Shows

Preparing for a Craft show

Top: Peardrop, Silver and Enamel Necklace, double-sided champleve. *Below:* Fish and Wave Rings, 8-10mm wide bands, Silver and Enamel by Rachel Gogerly.

Craft Shows

Another way to sell your work is 'direct' to the customer. This method avoids the need for a middle man (e.g. gallery/shop/website co-ordinator) or the costs of setting up your own showroom. It gives you the freedom to work from your own workshop, creating stock and then selling it for a commission free price.

Necklaces-Peardrop and Circular Neckwires, 40cm wires, Silver and Enamel, hand engraved and engine turned respectively by Rachel Gogerly, who has written the following article.

Craft Shows by Rachel Gogerly

Rachel Gogerly is a jeweller and an experienced Trade and Retail show exhibitor. She wrote this piece for the first edition of Second Steps, it is so comprehensive that it is still relevant and full of useful tips.

So you think you have got a good product and you want to exhibit at a show. But where do you start?'

There are many things to take into consideration and even if you have dealt with individual customers or shops and galleries before, shows are quite different. The right show can make or break a business. Exhibiting at a show is extremely hard work and requires a great deal of planning and preparation. Here are some pointers to help you on your way.

1. Choosing the right show for you and your product.

Exhibiting your work at an appropriate show is vital if you want to succeed. Think carefully about who you are aiming your work at - know who your customers are. Many shows are trade only and these shows are often big and attract buyers from all over the world. Trade orders can mean large orders, so think carefully if you can cope with producing your work in quantity.
Retail shows tend to attract a more local market. ✳ So consider who is likely to buy your work and is that type of buyer likely to attend that show.

✳ Research and more research,

Craft Shows by Rachel Gogerly

- Do your own market research and be confident about the type of customer who buys your work, it will help you select the right shows.

  From my experience, I would advise starting with a show that is not too big and one that can offer you a good learning ground. I chose a small stand at the well established British Craft Trade Fair in Harrogate (1987).
  At a trade fair you only need good samples of your work, because buyers place orders of what they see on your stand. This meant I didn't have to take masses of stock. The Harrogate Show attracts a lot of buyers from the North of UK and my initial orders were from small shops and galleries in quantities I could cope with easily. The show boosted my confidence and allowed me to expand my customer base. If you have never been to a show or don't know the difference between a Trade show and a Retail show **go and visit them.**

- Visit as many different shows as you can, all over the country, and always visit a show you are planning to do

- Always take a notepad and pen with you and be on the look out for work similar to yours

- Look at how it is displayed, how much it costs and ask if you can't see any prices

Craft Shows by Rachel Gogerly

However, don't make a nuisance of yourself, clutter a stand or get in the way of a genuine customer! It is as important to get to know your competitors as it is to know your customers. If your competitors are exhibiting at a particular show, then it may well be good for you to be there too. If you cannot find any work similar to yours, ask yourself why?

2 Preparations for a Show
2.1 Applying

Once you've decided which show is right for you to exhibit at, you will need to apply. Either telephone or write for application details, or ideally when visiting the show find out who the organisers are and if possible meet them and make yourself known, so they will send you an application at the appropriate time.

Some shows select their exhibitors and to apply for these shows it is essential that you submit **excellent images of your work.** Most committees that select work have very little time to view slides or photographs (often less than a minute), especially if it's a very popular show like the Chelsea Crafts Fair. I also know this from being on an advisory board for grant awards at Yorkshire and Humberside Arts. **It never ceased to amaze me how makers would apply for substantial grants with very poor quality images of their work.**

❋ The need for good photos again,

Craft Shows by Rachel Gogerly

2.2 Planning your Timetable

Once accepted for the show of your choice get yourself organised. You will only have between four to six months from the time of your application to the show itself.

- Put a year planner up on the wall.

- Mark on all the important dates you need to know, such as when to pay the balance of your stand costs, date for submitting slide and text for the catalogue.

- Then work out your own deadlines and mark those on too. e.g.when you want to send out invitations, and when you need to send work to the printers (business cards and other literature) so it is back in time for the show, and allocate time to plan your display.

By setting yourself a timetable you will hopefully avoid forgetting something and help yourself to keep a clear head as the show gets nearer and you get busier trying to finish all your work:

- take time to plan what you think you will need and decide what you can realistically make in the time available.

Craft Shows by Rachel Gogerly

- Think how much time you can dedicate to show work and how much time has to be given to existing orders.

New work is always good to have at any show. I have found new work should be started at least nine months in advance. This gives sufficient time for designing prototypes and the making of new pieces, as well as continuing with other on-going work. It may be that you think about new work even before you apply for a show, or straight after doing one, in preparation for the following year. If you do a show regularly, existing customers will always ask "What is new?" so make sure you have something to show them.

It is easy to put off making work for a show if you are already busy, but it is essential that you have your best work with you. Apart from anything else, it will give you more confidence. So get started as soon as you can and ensure your work is of the best quality whichever end of the market your work is aimed at. If you use sub-contractors it is all the more essential to be well organised because other people can let you down.

- **Over estimate the time you need.**

- Always make the big or most important pieces first, then if time does run out, it is easier to decide which smaller pieces can be left out.

Craft Shows by Rachel Gogerly

2.3 Handouts and literature for a show

Allow time to price every piece of work, during the last few days.

- Compile price lists and print plenty of copies.

- Do a stocklist, so you know exactly what you are taking with you.

- Use a laptop or PC to produce all your literature.

- Make sure all your handouts have all you contact details at the top.

Some customers do not buy at the show itself but will place an order later. Therefore it is essential that the information you hand out is clear and accurate and a good representation of your work. A good catalogue is useful as you'll find some buyers keep it to order from for the rest of the year.

- Get all you literature produced in good time, allowing at least six weeks for printing.

I use colour postcards as they give an impressive image of your work on one side and contact details on the other. People tend to keep postcards too, pinning them onto notice boards or standing them on mantles. If you are unsure about the type of literature that would be best for you, visit more shows and look at what other designer makers are doing.

Craft Shows by Rachel Gogerly

2.4 Displaying your Work

Do not leave decisions about your display until the setting up day.

- Schedule time well in advance to plan make and or buy your display.

Even when you are planning what work to take with you, you should be thinking how you will display it.

- Do you have a centre piece and how will you display it to catch the eye of a customer ?

As a precious metal jeweller, I realised very early on that I needed suitably secure show cases to display my work. A furniture designer, who had been recommended, designed and built me three showcases, each costing £500. It was a big investment at the time, but ten years on I'm still using them. We don't all need showcases, but choosing the appropriate display for your work is vital. Here are some points to consider when choosing your display:

- Its main function is to display your work, so it looks at its best and attracts customers,

- It should be made from materials that complement your work with good lighting,

- Should be sturdy so it doesn't fall down halfway through the show. Obvious but it does happen!

Craft Shows by Rachel Gogerly

- Make sure it is straight forward, fits your stand and doesn't take long to assemble and dismantle.

- Think about how you will transport it to the show and does it require protective wrapping.

- Work should be accessible. Customers may want to touch a piece, hold it or try it on.

- A storage area is always useful as part of a display to conceal extra stock, packaging materials such as boxes or bags and paperwork.

- It is also important to have a tidy, professional looking stand.

- Where will you complete your sales and orders? Is a simple clipboard sufficient or do you need an area to lean on for packaging etc.?

- Also think about where you will stand or sit. Try to stand most of the time, but not in front of your display and sit on a high stool rather than a low chair.

- Have a dry run i.e. set your display up marking out the size of your stand to check everything fits and looks good.

Craft Shows by Rachel Gogerly

- ❋ Read all the information from the organisers so you know what they provide, what you can hire as extras and what you can or cannot do to the stand e.g. some stand walls only allow velcro and not staple guns.

Do not assume anything about your stand, even if you have done the show before. Check everything, so you don't get any nasty surprises when you arrive. Some stands are literally the square metre floor space and may not include walls or fascia boards. In the case of marquees, there may not be a solid flooring but only uneven bare ground as the floor. Even with a shell scheme you will probably have to hire socket points for any extra lighting.

2.5 Point of Sale

Consider how you want to display your prices. Are you going to individually price items, have a list on view or include them as part of a catalogue handout? Whichever option you choose, ensure prices are typed and easy to read. Keep descriptions brief and clear, so customers can easily identify pieces of work.

Think about how you will present your work to a

❋ It is easy to be so busy preparing that you forget to actually read the instructions - take heed!

Craft Shows by Rachel Gogerly

customer if they ask to have a closer look at something. If your work is small and precious, present it on a fabric pad or tray. If it is displayed on one of the walls, make sure it is easy to remove and replace. Have a mirror available for items which can be tried on.

Packaging is very important and should be in keeping with the type of work you are selling. This is especially important at retail shows. As a jeweller I present my work in named boxes with named carrier bags too. Look into whether the organisers of the show provide any point of sale products which can be ordered in advance.

2.6 Mailing Lists

Consider building up a mailing list of your customers, especially if you plan to return to a show every year.

- Send invitations or leaflets about the show to existing customers and potential customers.

- Also enclose some of your own literature and remember to put on your stand number.

I send out between two to three hundred invites to an important show. Assembling all the envelopes is time consuming, so try to do it one evening, perhaps with friends and a bottle of wine, so it doesn't seem to take so long. I find my mailing list very worthwhile and worth the initial expense before a show.

- Monitor your own response rate; the key to a useful mailing list is to keep it up to date.

Craft Shows by Rachel Gogerly

2.7 Accommodation

If the show is too far from your home for you to commute, you will need to find accommodation.

- Book well in advance whether it is staying with friends or at an hostel or Bed & Breakfast.

Make sure you don't have much more than half an hours journey to and from the show each day and check bus and train times if you need to use them. You don't want to be late on the first day!

If you do stay with friends, make sure they know you'll be home late, need lots of baths/showers and will be tired. If you can stay with another stand holder it means you can travel together and you will both understand the ups and downs of exhibition life.

3 Setting Up

Setting up is always stressful and is especially so if it is the first show you have done. It can be quite daunting, walking into a large exhibition hall and seeing your stand for the first time. It can look very large and empty indeed. You know you only have few hours to make it look fantastic and all around you are other people busily assembling their displays, looking terribly calm and organised.I won't forget my first show, I was terrified and wanted to go home! It also seemed to take forever to set up, I was totally exhausted afterwards and the show hadn't even started! I now use a 'setting up

Craft Shows by Rachel Gogerly

day ' list, which includes items like screwdrivers, tape, ruler, scissors etc.

- Make your own (and add to it after each show, if you needed something you hadn't taken).

- Always check through your list prior to loading up the night before.

- Get a friend or colleague to help set up if possible.

If you have had a dry run of your display you will have a fairly good idea of what you will need. Take some food and drink for the day as you may not want to go out to get lunch or there may be limited or no facilities near by. Concentrate on your display and when you've finished go home and relax, don't stand around chatting and stopping others from getting on.

4 At the Show

Working at a show is tiring because you are on show too. In fact you are an integral part of your stand. So it is important that you are well presented, polite and approachable, by smiling. Speak to customers as they walk by, even if it is only to say 'Good morning". Selling your own work can sometimes be difficult because it is part of you. However, if you know your work is well made and like it, feel confident that others will too. Listen to what your customers say and be prepared to

Craft Shows by Rachel Gogerly

talk about your work, showing enthusiasm for what you do. Equally don't talk too much and be ready to close the sale at the appropriate moment. Don't ignore customers or stand chatting when customers are on your stand. Reading the paper, eating, sitting around looking fed up and leaving your stand unattended for long periods of time, makes you look unprofessional.

4.1 At Trade Fairs

When taking orders be realistic about your delivery dates, especially for large orders. Customers will cancel if you cannot keep to the dates, leaving the maker with no payment and half finished unwanted stock.

If a new customer places an order send a proforma invoice. However, on receipt of their cheque, ensure it clears through your bank before you send them your work. I have made that mistake myself once. I received a cheque, sent the work and then the cheque bounced. Luckily I lived near enough to go and ask for cash or my work back. I got my work back and not before time as the shop closed and went out of business shortly afterwards.

4.2 At retail shows

Selling work directly off your stand you will need back up stock; often the last day can be one of your busiest.

Craft Shows by Rachel Gogerly

- Have a cash box (with cash float to start you off),

- know what to check for when accepting cheques,

- look into having a credit card facility,

- make sure you have plenty of invoices & receipts.

Whatever type of show you exhibit at, be focused on what you want to achieve and if it helps you, set yourself a target. Despite the hard work, planning and preparation that is required to have a successful show, they can be fun too. They can be a great place to make new friends and catch up with old ones. Events like Exhibitors parties can be fun and useful for networking. Meals out and drinks with friends and other exhibitors are also enjoyable social occasions after a long day in the exhibition hall.

Finally, bear in mind you will be very tired after the show, so remember to give yourself a couple for days off before you embark on all those orders.

R.G.

www.rachelgogerly.co.uk

So many gems of wisdom are hidden within this article it is well worth taking time to read it carefully. It also endorses points made in other sections of the book.

Jeff Soan Case study

Jeff Soan graduated from Goldsmith's College, in the late 60's with a degree in Fine Art. After graduating he did a PGCE, and taught art for several years. In the 70's he had a family, changed careers and set up his own building business. It was not until the mid-80's that Jeff decided it was time to leave his building days behind. Partly due to knee and back troubles but also through a need to be involved once again in a creative environment.

Jeff was about to take a job as an art technician at Oxford Polytechnic, when a chance encounter with a wobbly rat from Chile, made him think twice. The wobbly rat in question belonged to a friend and was an articulated folk toy. He was so taken with this rat that he did not start the job at Oxford Poly. Instead he joined and passed a City and Guilds course in toy making at the London College of Furniture.

After which, in 1987, he set up a workshop in his garden shed, selling the toys which he made at a local market in Greenwich. Although it was hard work, Jeff describes the three enjoyable market years as an excellent lesson in self-promotion:

Jeff Soan Case study

"People say that makers are not usually good at selling and promoting their own work. I think this is partly true, I am guilty myself of pointing out faults in the work rather than the virtues. On the other hand no one really knows the work like the maker, the creative impulses behind it and the knowledge accumulated by working closely with materials for many years. I think people would rather meet the maker, however inept, than the most accomplished salesperson."

There were two significant turning points in Jeff's career. The first was when a TV producer, who was making a programme for the BBC called 'Handmade', spotted him at the market selling wobbly fish. Jeff appeared on the programme and shortly afterwards his sales escalated. It was around this time that he started to make a large variety of wobbly wooden toys.

The second turning point was in 1991 when his application to The Chelsea Craft Fair, organised by the Crafts Council, was accepted. "I had applied to The Chelsea Craft Fair for a few years with no success. Then I invested in ✳ some professional photos of my work and that year I got in. This may have been a coincidence but I think the panels there, are looking at thousands of images and they will tend to throw out poorly

✳ Once again the importance of good photographs and perseverance are emphasised.

Jeff Soan Case study

focused, badly lit, amateur slides no matter how beautiful the work."

Exhibiting at Chelsea provided great exposure for Jeff, both nationally and internationally and he continues to exhibit there today. He also uses the website as a means of promotion. "These days a website is an obvious way to present ourselves. I've found it incredibly useful as an online brochure, which can be updated regularly. I've tried to keep it clear and simple, using but not over using the technology." Due to high demand Jeff has a part-time assistant and sells his wobbly wooden toys worldwide - particularly in Germany, Japan and the USA. **www.**wobblywood.demon.co.uk   J.S.

Craft shows

Art in Action,
The Organiser
96 Sedlescombe Road
Fulham
SW6 1RB
T: 020 7381 3192
E: info@artinaction.org.uk
www.artinaction.org.uk
An annual July event at Waterperry House, Wheatley
near Oxford, first held in 1976, this is now one of the
largest shows of craft demonstrations in the UK.

Art in Clay
Andy Mcinnes **T** 01494 450504
9 Ivy Grove
Carlton
Nottingham
NG41RG
E: newexhibitor@ArtinClay.co.uk
www.hdevents.co.uk
Annual ceramic exhibition at Hatfield House, Herts.

Brighton Craft Fair
PO Box 73
Hove
BN3 1ZE
E: info@brightoncraftfair.co.uk
www.brightoncraftfair.co.uk

Craft shows

British Craft Trade Fair (Harrogate)
www.bctf.co.uk   See advert page 221

Ceramic Art London
E: organisers@ceramics.org.uk
www.ceramics.org.uk
An annual event presented by the Craft Potters
Association in association with the Crafts Council at
the Royal College of Art, London
Application deadline September.

The Chelsea Craft Show is moving,
from Oct 2006 it is to be held at:
Somerset House
Strand
WC2
Still organised by the Crafts Council apply on-line,
entry via selection approx six months earlier.
www.craftscouncil.org.uk

Craft in Focus
PO Box 942
Maidstone
ME15 0YB
T: 01622 747325
E: info@craftinfocus.com
www.craftinfocus.com
4 events - check details

Craft shows

Dazzle
PO Box 36
Cranbrook
TN17 2DF
T 01580 852503
www.zone-d.com
Jewellery only-please check web site for more details.

Design Edge
www.design-edge.uk.com   See advert page 227

Eastern Events Ltd.
Diggins Farm House
Buxton Road
Aylsham
NR11 6UB
T: 01263 734711
E: info@easternevents.com
www.easternevents.com

The Knitting and Stitching Show
Creative Exhibitions Ltd
8 Greenwich Quay
Clarence Road
SE8 3EY
T: 0208 692 2299
www.twistedthread.com

Craft shows

Living Crafts
66 Penny Street
Portsmouth
T: 02392 863871
E: webinfo@livingcrafts.co.uk
www.livingcrafts.co.uk
Largest and longest running show in Europe - in 27th
year, held at Hatfield House, Herts.

PSM Ltd ✳ see adverts pages 221 & 227
Hammonds Barn
London Road
Burgess Hill
RH15 9QJ
T: 01444 246446
E: info@bctf.co.uk
www.bctf.co.uk

n.a.m.e.
New Artists and Makers Emporium
PO Box 4042
Rugby
CV21 9AW
T: 01403 260389
E: enquiries@artistsand makers.net
www.artistsandmakers.net
Interesting website with conveyor belt of makers
images, click on one and their email pops up.

Craft shows

One Year On
Organised by Crafts Council
T: 0207 806 2529
E: m_bowen@craftscouncil.org.uk
Annual selling exhibition, part of The New Designers
Graduate Show, exhibitors must be within one year of
graduating or within one year of being in business.

Orchard Events Ltd.
Pond House,
1 Priory Road,
Kew Green,
TW9 3TQ
T: 020 8332 9595
E: orchardevents01@aol.com
www.festivegiftfair.
Organises two popular Christmas consumer gift shows.

Pulse (May)
Earls Court
E: neil.gaisford@clarionevents.com
www.pulse-london.com
An internationalexhibition for lifestyle and interior
accessories - with particular interest in promoting
new designers.

Spectrum (Interior Design incl furniture)
Contact David Field **T:** 020 8943 9788

design edge

...cutting edge

Every September

Sandown Park
Exhibition Centre
Esher, Surrey, UK.

www.design-edge.uk.com

'London's contemporary
home and gift fair for
UK makers'

Craft shows

Top Drawer (September)
Grand Hall Olympia
& Top Drawer (January)
Earls Court
T: 020 7370 8324
E: topdrawer@clarionevents.com
www.topdrawer.co.uk

Twist Art & Design
Redloh House
2 Michael Road
London
SW6 2AD
T: 020 7371 7303
www.twistand design.co

100% Design Show
Reed Exhibition Companies
Oriel House
26 the Quadrant
Richmond
Twickenham TW9 1DL
T: 020 8910 7724
E: :chuffelmann@reedexpo.co.uk
www.100percentdesign.co.uk

Exhibiting abroad

As John Mckellar points out, in the following article, it is best to gain experience by exhibiting in British Trade Shows before attempting to launch yourself abroad.

There are many extra problems attached to foreign shows, language and currency being the main ones. Plus travelling, packaging and delivery, insurance and follow up orders. However the internet simplifies many of these difficulties and banks can easily arrange Telegraphic Transfers in any currency

If you are interested in showing your work abroad ✳ UK Trade & Investment can offer a great deal of information and support. Being part of a 'Trade Mission' is a good way to start as you benefit from the back up and promotion of the organisers.

They will provide details about the shows with which they are involved. There is a scheme SESA - Support for Exhibition and Seminars Abroad, details of which are available on their website.

✳ UK Trade & Investment
T: 020 7215 8000
www.uktradeinvest.gov.uk

Exhibiting abroad by John McKellar

John McKellar, *jeweller and Gallery owner who wrote earlier about the pros and   of running a retail outlet, (see p193) here points out the pros and cons of exhibiting at overseas trade shows.*

There are opportunities to show at foreign trade shows with funding support from the UK Trade & Investment via sponsors, such as the Crafts Council or Chambers of Commerce. Generally travel costs are paid, and exhibition costs may be subsidised.

Pros:
- Expands potential market,

- Seeing developments, in your field abroad, can be very stimulating,

- You may be able to combine your trip with sight seeing or a holiday,

- It may raise your international profile,

- Showing with a group can be fun socially.

Cons:
- May be harder to establish a presence in market, due to unfamiliarity and language problems,

- Can be harder to chase outstanding payments,

Exhibiting abroad by John McKellar

- Bureaucratic complications with customs etc., shipping orders abroad may be complicated and differing business styles may problems.

This is not something to undertake until you have had experience of showing at British Trade Shows, and of supplying overseas customers. Unless you have already saturated your home market your resources are usually better concentrated on British buyers. It can be stimulating and some crafts may have a thriving overseas market. It is worth researching the market thoroughly before you go; consider using the market report service available through British Consulates.

Try to go a few days before the show to research the market 'on the ground' and allow a few days to stay after the show finishes for follow-up (much harder to do once you return home). Take plenty of literature with you, it may be harder to replace abroad if you run out.

I think you would be very brave to go on your own unless you have knowledge or contacts it is better to be part of a group, the chance of going on a sponsored mission is well worth considering if you are established enough to be able to make use of it.

J.M.

Direct Selling via Internet

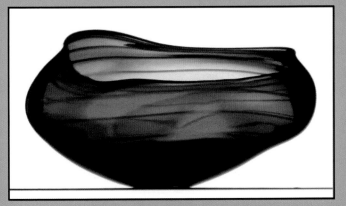

Glass bowl by Layne Rowe

Internet selling

Marketing is not just advertising. It includes every method of selling and promotion. Many of these are covered in other sections of this book i.e. selling through galleries, trade and retail shows, exhibitions and commissions. In other words any way of bringing your work to the attention of potential buyers which includes selling on the internet.

Since the first edition of Second Steps was published, in 1998, the internet has become an essential ingredient in the marketing package. Nearly every business now has an Email address and a website to refer to.

A large number of online galleries/markets, which opened during the last few years, have since closed. However there are some who have grown in stature and many new ones who have appeared to take the place of the first runners. Many of these sites are focusing on selling crafts direct to the public. Every new maker should at least consider the advantages offered by these opportunities. Especially as many of the sites are offering free entry and taking a low commission on any sales made, in order to get their sites launched with a wide selection of work.

Once you have a page set up, either on your own or under the umbrella of an internet gallery, you have just dipped your toe into the vast pool of the internet. The biggest challenge is to persuade the public to browse your site and to be intrigued enough to find out more or even better, to place an order.

Internet selling

If you have taken space with one of the commercial sites they should be marketing hard on your behalf. Some will advertise widely in relevant magazines and on the Internet itself, to introduce customers. Leaving you free to create the work to sell. Others may not be so conscientious - **be selective in your choice.**

If you decide to create you own site, it may well be worth employing a designer or at least taking advice from an expert to help achieve a distinctive, simple but eye catching site. The experts should also have the knowledge to contact all the main search engines with the relevant key link words.

Once again the choice of image is important, the work should be something which you can provide repeats of, when orders roll in. If you are scanning your own images it is not necessary to scan at high resolution, 300 dpi will be sufficient as the majority of monitors only display the images at 72dpi. If you are joining a group site one which has a selection process would be best, so that the discerning viewer willfeel that they have entered a quality site.

Useful sites when web designing:
www.nic.uk.   (registering names)
www.registername.co.uk (self-explanatory)
www.paypal.co.uk (to set up on-line sales)
www.reason8.com (basic DIY)

Web Design by Andy Green-Howard

Andrew Green-Howard wrote a piece about designing web pages in the last edition, at that time he was a part-time web-designer working mainly for artists. Although his teaching commitments have taken over I include an edited version of his piece as he made many useful points.

It is vital to be totally clear as to what you want from a website. Artists make things, things to be looked at, handled, used and enjoyed. However, art is primarily about communicating, whether it is through a beautiful pot, a piece of jewellery or a more 'conventional' work of art, hung on a wall.

The internet is also about communication, mainly entertainment or exchanging information and goods/services. Having a 'web presence' must now be seen as an essential step for anyone wishing their artistic output to have more than just a periodic, parochial airing. The only question left is - how?:

Joining a gallery:

A large number of galleries have websites. There are many 'gallery sites' that exist only on the net. Their purpose is solely to sell items. Most will require images of your work along with a small C.V. and statement. In return they will promote your work, taking a commission on all sales.

Having your own website:

One disadvantage of being part of a 'corporate' image is anonymity on the web. Being part of a larger website,

Web Design by Andy Green-Howard

you have no control over the style of the site, nor is it likely that someone searching the internet for you would find you, unless they knew the web address beforehand. Both of these disadvantages are overcome by having your own website. You have a say in the design and style of the site, and if the web address has your name in it, your presence and 'findability' increases.

However you never get something for nothing, and creating your own website is not a task to be tackled unless you have had training. When choosing a web designer, use the same criteria you would to select a postcard printer: credentials and cost

When you have found someone, ask to see examples of work which they have done for others.

• Have they worked for artists/makers before? (This is important—most web designers will compromise on quality/number of images to make a slick site, whereas makers want quality images). Anyone with a computer could set up as a web designer, so ask:

• Have they professional affiliations?

• Have they any awards for previous websites?

• How much will they charge?

A basic website should cost about the same as a postcard run, rising with complexity, unless you want online sales added to your site. Some web designers will

Web Design by Andy Green-Howard

advertise low prices, but then add 'extras' such as recognisable web addresses, e-mail, etc. Some will even expect you to provide your own digital images.
Ask what is included, the minimum you should expect to receive is:

- a decent/relevant web address

- an e-mail address

- submission to search engines

- the ability to supply your images to the designer

Selling work online.
There are very few companies who are making money through selling online. This does not mean that you won't make money from your site – if the site is advertised well, who knows what may happen. True stories include UK artists contacted by American galleries wanting to ship work out to sell. Commissions for work through seeing the quality of the artist's work on the website and contacts made as far afield as Sri Lanka. However, direct selling should not be your first priority when thinking about the internet.

Final thoughts
You should consider the internet in the same breath as getting a postcard printed. The only question is:

Web Design by Andy Green-Howard

How do you make the effort to get yourself associated with a gallery website and check that?

- your work will always be on display?

- the 'pedigree' of the gallery is good?

- how well they sell?

- how big is their mailing list?

Or do you go for the individual route?
If so take time to find a good web designer who will create quality and success for your site.

Once you have a site, ✳ publicise it. Make sure that the web address appears on any printed material which you give to anyone. Also check that your designer is submitting the website to search engines regularly. If you create your own site try to arrange a link or hyperlink with any gallery with whom you exhibit.

You should always check that your web address is registered. If you are using a web designer, ask. They should register it automatically. If you are creating your own site, then whoever you bought the address from (usually ISP) should register it for you, once again, check! **www**.nic.uk

✳ Like Kathleen Hills who even prints her website on the base of every piece of work she produces.

Web Design by Andy Green-Howard

Whenever images are placed on the internet there is always the risk that someone will take your image and use it to their advantage. **Always make sure that there is a copyright notice on the first page of your site**, to protect your rights. You can add copyright watermarks to your images, but to be effective, you will need to purchase a copyright identifier, which will usually cost upwards of £100 per year. This tracks your images, notifying you if they are copied from your website. Again, if you are using a designer, ask them if they offer this, and what they charge for the service. However, only you can decide whether the identifier is worth the money.

Finally, remember that although you may not understand the internet, it is just another marketplace. However you enter this market place, make sure that you are happy with what you get and that it gives the right impression of your work. People will judge you by your web presence. The number of sites is huge – even a poorly advertised website can expect over one hundred visits per month and well publicised ones are getting that daily!

The UK registering body is called Nominet and their website address is **www.nic.uk.** Here you can check to see if an address is registered and if so what to do.

Internet notes + Offer

The following sites are just a selection of those who offer opportunities to sell your work. They all have different ways of charging, make sure that you check all their terms before deciding to take part.

www.britishcrafts.co.uk

www.craft-connections.com

www.craftselect.co.uk

www.design-gap.co.uk

www.newdesignersonline.co.uk

www.photostore.org.uk (Crafts Council site)

N.B. ※

I am very interested to know how successful websites are at selling crafts. If any readers have experience of either selling or receiving commissions, as a result of their website presence, please **let me know**.

I am equally interested to receive general feedback on how useful (or not) this book is in your research. Constructive suggestions about areas which should be included or developed further would also be useful. ED

※ All those who reply will be entered into a draw-the winner will receive a **free page** in the Second Steps Portfolio. If there are sufficient replies coming in, on a regular basis there will be an annual draw-so even if you are reading this book in 2008 it is still worth writing in. Contact details at front of book and on: www.bcfbooks.co.uk

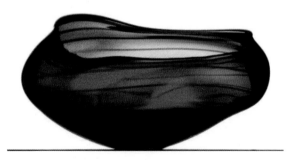

Internet - Glass for the Present

Glass for the Present was established in March 2005 by Robyn West. The business specialises in selling the work of British glass artists and creating an online gallery was a key part of the business.

Many businesses expect that once they have a website, orders will just come rolling in. Not so. A website is just another marketing tool and needs to be promoted in the normal way in order that people may know about it. This was well understood by Robyn, who shares here the key planning decisions.

Products are sold on the basis of being made to order, ie the business keeps only a small selection of stock for display purposes. Recognising that this could be an obstacle to sales, it was decided from the outset that the website had to be of a high standard in order to project the right image of the business, and to give visitors the best photographs and information possible to attract orders.

Delivery and packaging also needed careful consideration. As most goods are made to order, the website needed to indicate the anticipated waiting time for purchases. Customers' orders are received by Robyn and forwarded to the artist. Once the glass is produced, it is sent direct to the customer by the artist on Robyn's behalf. She had her own packing tape produced (including logo and contact details) which the artists use for all Glass for the Present dispatches. Customers then recognise the delivery as having come from Glass for the Present, which completes the buying-cycle. The risk for safe arrival of goods rest with the artist, whose responsibility it is to ensure glass is packaged carefully."

The next major decision was who would build the website? The self-build route was much cheaper, but limiting and time-consuming. She decided to have it built to her specification, which was more expensive, but she is very proud of the end result. The site also complies with current legislation. Any major changes do incur costs but these are managed carefully.

In designing the website, she put herself in the shoes of the visitor and created a flowchart of the whole process, which helped to identify practical issues she hadn't thought about. Visiting other websites and noting the positive and negative aspects of navigating them was also useful.

Robyn investigated the cost of an online payment system. She decided that until she could be confident the level of sales would cover the costs, it was too great an expense. She was fortunate, however, to be able to hire a mobile credit card unit from a local arts organisation and can therefore offer credit payment by telephone, which is a happy compromise.

Legislation was quite a headache. Businesses must now comply with the Disability Discrimination Act, and this includes accessibility to websites. Failure to comply may incur a hefty fine if caught. Consumers' rights are

Internet - Glass for the Present

also well protected, so getting to grips with the Distance Selling Regulations and Sale of Goods Act was important, especially being clear about the process for returned products.

Since the launch, Robyn keeps a close eye on the monthly website statistics, which provide valuable information about the effectiveness of the website. She has also learnt about Search Engine Optimisation, which is a complex and constantly changing issue, and believes the only assured way of getting people to your website is by promoting your business in the traditional way.

Keeping the website fresh is vital. Updating information once a month helps with search engine rankings, and also encourages visitors to return regularly. Robyn says there is still some reluctance by consumers to buy art on the internet, but believes the trend is changing for the better. The huge number of compliments about her glass and the website give Robyn confidence that as her business profile and customer base grow, her website will be an increasingly important tool in the success of her business.   *Robyn West*

www.consumerdirect.gov.uk
Business Link offer courses (often free) on building a website, internet marketing and search engine optimisation
Department of Trade & Industry: Sale of Goods Act and Distance Selling Regulations

Manufacturing

Case studies:

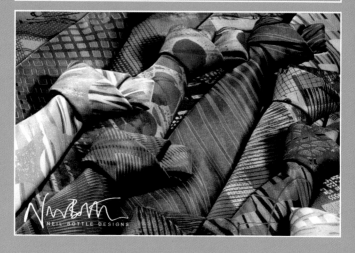

NEIL BOTTLE DESIGNS

Sara Harris Manufacturing case study

Selling a design to a manufacturing company-Sara Harris shares her experiences.

Prior to the completion of my course I entered a jewellery competition in Germany As a result of winning the competition I was approached by a large German jewellery manufacturing company, who were interested in buying my winning design. Having, obviously, never encountered this kind of interest before I set about researching how to approach, respond and deal legally with this type of proposal.

I rang everyone I could think of, teachers, designers, membership organisations and copyright issuers. One past teacher gave essential help on how to word my letters legally but no one organisation could tell me exactly how to proceed, what to expect financially or what to ask for.

With the invaluable support of a past lecturer, the first step was to make my initial written response. I replied that I was interested in hearing their proposal. This resulted in the company requesting a sample of the design, for their design team to assess, with regards to commercial viability and manufacture possibilities. This sample was sent with an accompanying letter outlining:

Sara Harris Manufacturing case study

- the commercial confidence in which it was sent

- stating copyright ownership of the design and any variations on the theme of which the design was based i.e. variations on scale, materials and usage (rings, earrings, bangles).

As the awards ceremony was held in Germany I was able to travel to Europe. At the same time I arranged to meet the president of the company interested in my design. This resulted in my being invited to visit the company and discuss their proposal. I flew over and was treated to an invaluable tour of the company premises. This enabled me to view the company ethos at first hand and to see their manufacturing departments. I'm sure this is quite rare but it gave me confidence that my design was going to be produced and represented in a way with which I was happy. I was invited to become involved in the selection process of the finalised design and to discuss, with their design team, elements of the designs success which were important to me as the designer.

This left me feeling that my views, as the designer, were valued and important to them and it was very interesting and exciting to be included in the whole process. I have heard stories of designs being sold and then changed so dramatically, by the manufacturers, that the design is unrecognisable. Often not what

Sara Harris Manufacturing case study

the designer would like to be credited with at all.

The company wanted to buy my design outright. In other words they would be entitled to produce the design indefinitely, while crediting me as the designer in any publicity. As the designer I was offered a percentage of royalties, based on the number of items sold, for as long as the item was manufactured, payment being made twice a year. In addition an initial payment was paid on completion of the contract. Being a large company they had a standard contract and percentage paid and there was little room for negotiation on my behalf.

Every situation is different but I went out to meet the company at an obvious disadvantage. Each letter of correspondence from me had been guided by my lecturer. Whilst I was involved in the design elements, when it came to financial discussion, I was not realistically experienced enough to negotiate. It seems that the company concerned were an exception to the norm, in terms of the treatment and involvement I was given in the process.

The end result was a positive one but I was left feeling that I had really not a leg to stand on, against this huge manufacturing company, in terms of what was a 'Standard' contract.

My contract was quite straight forward, it simply stated:

- the parties involved,

Sara Harris Manufacturing case study

- a specific description of the design elements being bought (including variations on the theme),

- my right to be credited as the designer on all publicity,

- percentage paid, when, on what price (wholesale or retail) and in what currency.

Given that I had already seen first hand, the type of manufacturing techniques which they implemented and how they intended to produce the design, this seemed enough. However in hindsight, had the company been one that was being negotiated with from a distance and with an unknown reputation, there are other points which would have been important to consider.

- A sample of the finished piece prior to agreement,

- a clause protecting the designers right to approve this as a representation of his/her work,

- clauses pertaining to what happens to the ownership of the design should the company cease to produce it, due to either lack of viability or bad manufacturing methods.

Sara Harris Manufacturing case study

- I also learned that, had my design not been in the public arena already, I could have negotiated a higher percentage. On the basis that the design could then have been patented by the company.

I'm sure this is not a situation that arises regularly, particularly to someone with so little experience. However it made me aware that there is no one advisory body to provide this kind of advice and support to individuals just starting out. Unless of course you are prepared to pay high membership charges. One resource that has since been of invaluable help is the Artists' Newsletter website, for standard blank outlines, on a variety of contracts. I wish I had had access to it at the time, as it gives a good starting point for a number of important legal clauses. This also underlined for me the importance of being able to access the internet. I could have prepared business wise for the meeting and also have done my homework on the company!

Hopefully this article will at least give an example of one such situation. I was lucky that the company, with which I was dealing, were extremely honest, had an excellent business ethos and had a well established reputation, as I have heard many horror stories. Nerve wracking as it was, selling designs to manufacturing companies is an excellent way of getting your work to a wider audience and starting to earn an income.

SH

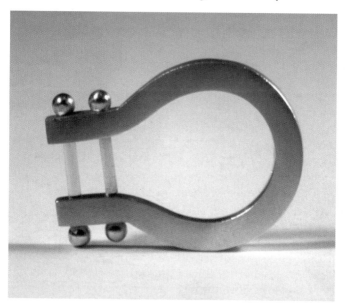

Kathleen Hills Manufacturing case study

Kathleen Hills graduated from St. Martins and went on to do an MA at the Royal College before launching her business 'Multi' in 2002. Here she shares her experiences of working in the manufacturing field.

www.multidesign.info

Kathleen had a very successful university career and when she moved on to study for her MA chose to spend the second year in industry. The world of manufacturing was already familiar to her as her father was a manufacturer, so moulds around the house, visits to foundries were nothing unusual for Kathleen having grown up within an active small family business.

She was lucky to gain a placement with Wedgwood where she was able to develop her own designs to a point where they were ready for production. Armed with samples Kathleen spent one day a week visiting other manufacturers in the Stoke area to discuss production of her work.

In this way she met a variety of businesses, saw how they worked; how they treated new young makers and discovered what they would charge. She quickly realised how important it was to have really good relationship with your manufacturer. She did not immediately find the right one; one company didn't take her seriously and another wasn't able to cope with her contemporary designs.

However she eventually found a small family business with whom she has built a very good relationship. They are willing to be flexible and can deal with small or large orders. Now that she is established with them Kathleen sometimes discusses a new design, when it is still on the drawing board, so that they can advise if it is practical and get an idea of the approximate price. This way she knows, before she has spent too much time on the project, if it will be viable.

She generally orders about ten different items to be made in batches of different quantities, making about 100 pieces in all. She then keeps some of each design for stock and fulfils orders with the rest.✳ **One very good idea she has is to have her website printed on the base of each item.** Kathleen finds that designing and creating a new piece can be a long process, sometimes taking up to around six months.

During the second year of running 'Multi' Kathleen was awarded a Craft Council Development award. She had been interviewed for one the previous year but was unlucky. On reflection Kathleen felt that she had taken too varied a selection of samples and had insufficient time to talk the interviewers through her work.

Kathleen also entered work for various awards and was short-listed for the Peugeot Design Award in 2001, which she has found useful in raising her profile.

✳ The advice to put your website on everything is taken to new levels by Kathleen, and means that her contact details are constantly available to the buyer.

Kathleen Hills Manufacturing case study

She does not use an agent or distributor relying on her own research and ingenuity to find outlets. She finds that her work sells best through designer shops rather than galleries, but regularly attends craft shows like Pulse, Top Drawer, the Chelsea Crafts Fair and 100% Design which she finds the most successful. Kathleen finds these shows very good for introducing her to new suppliers, she also finds her very well designed web-site is efficient in bringing in new orders.✳ **She always carries a small sample piece with her, in her bag or pocket, just in case she meets someone who could offer a suitable sales opportunity.** This way she managed to get her milk jug design used in the window display at Paul Smith's in Covent Garden - a real coup. (Illustration page 257)

Now that she has several years experience she has also started teaching, giving lectures about Professional Development. This new side to her career helps to balance her work and give it a new dimension. Kathleen has obviously paced herself well, not taking on too much too soon which has helped create her success.

✳ Ingenuity and thinking laterally is the most effective sales method.

Kathleen Hills Manufacturing case study

Points for a new maker to consider on seeking and approaching a manufacturer:

- Research thoroughly first

- Find names by contacting universities in the area where you hope to find the manufacturer

- Search through yellow pages or **www**.yel.com

- Telephone to arrange a meeting, then visit about six manufacturers with drawings and prototype

- Discuss every aspect with them and make clear how you hope to be working, what quantities you have in mind and how you see your future

- Get estimates although you may not be deciding on the cheapest but rather the one that you feel is most compatible with your way of working.

- Negotiate payment,this may be cash with order to start with, but will evolve as you build trust

K.H.

Milkii: *Bone china milk jug with set of foil tops in various colours and one set of re-sealable red plastic lids*

Bone china strings of lights: *can be displayed as bunches or trailed along walls or ceilings on little hooks*

Neil Bottle Case study

Neil Bottle, who studied at Middlesex University, has been working with textiles for 18 years. During this time he has built up a very successful name for himself. First designing and making an in-house range of limited edition textile accessories and now working with new technology to create designs for the British Museum and Globe Theatre shops.

Neil's career started at one of the first New Designers Shows in 1989, where he was an award winner. This helped attract attention to his stand and resulted in approaches from a number of companies including Harrods and Liberty. As he says buyers from large companies are always keen to find raw new talent, they hope to buy-in a few designs which can then be tweaked, by their in-house designers, and used in their own ranges.

The award which Neil had won provided cash which helped him rent and equip his first work-shop in London. Also, almost more importantly, he was supplied with business back up. This meant that he was in a position to show his work, on a group stand, at the next Decorex Show. He had been advised that no one should show there unless they had a workshop ready, in which to undertake any orders obtained. He was put in touch with an agent who luckily dealt with all the paper work connected with orders for home and abroad. As this

Neil Bottle Case study

included shipping and exporting, Neil, on his own, would have been out of his depth, at this stage in his career.

Neil continued to work in his rather basic workshop, hand-painting and screen-printing for the first year. He built up many contacts, gained much experience and then decided to return to his home county of Kent.

In a large well equipped workshop orders continued to come in thick and fast. The business was boosted by taking space at Chelsea Crafts Fair for ten consecutive years. It evolved into a family business with Neil's wife and mother helping with some of the processes. Of course it is not just the creation of the actual orders that has to be considered. As Neil reminds us there is the labelling, packaging and delivery to be researched. It is all very well being creative and coming up with original, exciting designs; each will need a new box or alternative packaging solution before it can be sent to the shop. Hunting out the best packing for a new piece can be very time consuming. Neil also advises on the importance of thinking through the delivery process, if shipping is required what papers will be needed for customs and insurance?

In 1996, when their first child arrived, Neil's wife felt she no longer had time to continue helping in the work-shop, so he had to become an employer, always a big step for a small business. Six years on he employs up to five employees, depending on the work in hand. He uses a large number of out-workers and specialist companies

Neil Bottle Case study

for particular finishes or items

Neil has received many orders from the Far East, supplying a large store with designer clothes and accessories, where expense seems no problem. He recounts how he prepared an order for 250 hand painted cushions covers, which he planned to deliver unfilled. However the company wanted all the feathers to be inserted before they left England- regardless-knowing their large mark-up could cover the costs.

One of Neil's most exciting orders was to supply goods for the Millennium Dome. He was given an amazing order for over 2,500 items in July 1999. However, due to their complete lack of organisational skills, they would not finalise the order and did not do so until November. Apparently they did at least realise that not all the items would be needed at once, which was lucky, as the order was not completed until May 2000. Neil had, of course, agreed a price for the whole job, and given a discount for quantity, way back in July. He admits that he did not do sufficient research, as too late he discovered that the packaging alone would cost £2,500. As a result he is far more cautious now.

Neil made several very important points to consider before taking on large orders or becoming involved in the world of manufacturing:

- Do you **really** want to make large quantities. Small orders are good too, you can be responsive to individual requirements.

Neil Bottle Case study

- If their order is late a company can refuse to accept it (if abroad this could involve you in shipping it home).
- When estimating check if there will be special delivery requirements or loading difficulties.
- Don't be over optimistic and take on too much.
- Try to see problems from the other persons' point of view.
- Don't be impressed by big names, keep your feet on the ground and think carefully before taking on new orders.
- Be open to new ideas and think laterally.
- All work and no play is no fun,
- keep some time to be creative .

NEIL BOTTLE DESIGNS

Neil Bottle Case study

While Neil continues to work in his chosen field he is aware that trade patterns have changed over the years. He believes that a period spent working as a designer for a company, could be a very useful experience, before setting up an individual workshop. He also thinks that designers should not be 'too precious' about their designs, if an agent or buyer is willing to buy one of your designs, outright, go for it.

However not many will be as lucky as Sara Harris (p251) and able to retain the copyright. Neil has noticed a shake up of trends in trading in the Retail World since the mid '90's He feels it is now a cut throat business, as companies in the Far East employ good, often British, designers, get the work made up by cheap labour then sell it for large profits. The British workshop, with British overheads, is being squeezed out of business as imports are a real threat.

P.S 2006 Three years later, Neil is now spending much of his time working with new technology, including creating his designs on the computer and experimenting with dye chemistry. He has had some exciting commissions with The Globe Theatre and the British Museum, (the latter discovered him from a random search on the internet). Neil has enjoyed the challenge of working with these companies to create interesting and authentically correct merchandising for their respective shops. This means he is doing far fewer big runs, preferring to concentrate on this original work.

Neil Bottle Case study

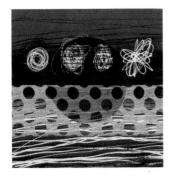
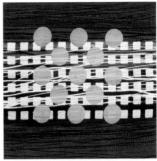

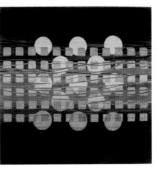

Photos by Greg Bottle

Jo Mitchell Case study

Jo Mitchell started up her company 'Hotmetal Contemporary Jewellery' in 1990. From 1982-85, she trained at the Bath Academy of Art studying Graphic Design and Visual Communication. In the few years following graduation she worked as a graphic designer for a major UK company and also set up a greeting card business with a friend, importing designs from Japan. During this time Jo enrolled on a part-time Adult Education course in jewellery and silversmithing.

Today she is based in Bath and with the help of her husband and brother-in-law, Hotmetal has been running as a successful business for 16 years. With a great deal of experience and advice to offer, Jo believes that talking directly to possible buyers is the most effective means of selling work.

"We started Hotmetal during the height of the recession, which was quite good as things couldn't exactly get worse. Shops were closing down all the time whereas now we are constantly meeting people who are opening new galleries. When I started out I probably contacted about 50 galleries and shops. I spoke to the buyers about my work, arranged to send a photo or samples, then followed up with a call later. It can be an advantage to contact companies directly—at least you

Jo Mitchell Case study

get a chance to speak to the actual buyer and find out what they are looking for."

It was around this time that Jo had the opportunity of exhibiting at the Birmingham NEC Spring Fair, where she was given a one foot square space on the 'Design Gap' stand. As she points out, 'being on a shared stand with other makers is a great way to reduce the costs of showing at a trade fair'. Even better quite a few orders were placed during the show. Jo still exhibits at trade fairs and tries to attend three a year.

Her first big break came when a buyer for Liberty bought all that Jo had and then ordered more. "I heard that the Regent Street branch of Liberty had a 'British Craft' department (this has since closed). I made an appointment to see the buyer and showed him my jewellery. It fitted in well with the style of the department at the time and he placed a good order."

As well as Liberty, Jo has also supplied Selfridges, the Royal Academy of Art, the National Trust and the Guggenheim Museum in New York.

"We provide galleries and shops with smart photographic point-of-sale cards to display with the jewellery. These give the work an identity and also show a wider range of available designs. We also do CV sheets for shops to give to customers."

Early on I decided I wanted to supply shops and galleries rather than individual private customers. Making volume orders always appealed to me, rather

Jo Mitchell Case study

than one-off special commissions. This was a significant decision and it dictated how the business should grow. As is the case with most makers, Jo has had to learn along the way but apart from perhaps investing in some specialist tools at an earlier stage and having a little more training, she generally would not alter much if starting again. Her work recently appeared in Vogue magazine, so Jo's self-promotion skills are obviously still in good working order. As she says, 'running a business does require a genuine love of what you are doing and dedication but is most definitely worth the effort.'

J.M.

Jane Charles Case study

From 1981-83 Jane Charles studied a
multi-disciplinary art and design course
at North Staffordshire Polytechnic and
specialised in glass. After graduating
she enrolled on 'The Dudley Course', a
one year, factory-based course, run by
studio glass-makers. She found this
particularly useful because it focused
very much on the technical side of
glass-blowing. The experience she gained has proved to
be invaluable throughout her career.

From 1984-87 Jane worked at various glass-workshops
to gain further experience. As she points out she was not
in a position to set up on her own at that stage.
However, in 1987 Jane did establish her own glass
studio in Edinburgh which she transferred to Newcastle-
upon-Tyne in 1990, where she is still based today.

When she first set up Jane had the benefit of a small
grant from Edinburgh County Council. With the grant
aid she bought some equipment and rented a small
studio on the outskirts of Edinburgh. The studio had no
gas or electricity, both had to be installed at a further
cost. Jane admits that she took the studio more for its
location and did not really consider the impracticalities.
Jane stresses that to get a business up and running,
keeping costs as low as possible has to be a top priority:
"To avoid the expense of equipment when setting up,
think about hiring studios, that way you can book a set

Jane Charles Case study

amount of time, go in, work flat out and then walk away without having all the ongoing costs."

Another way of keeping out-goings to a minimum is to be selective when trying to sell work:
"Rather than spending lots of money on trade shows, target certain galleries instead and arrange to go and see them with a selection of work. Pick an area of the country and then arrange a series of appointments. That way you have their full attention."

The emergence of interior design programmes and magazines in the late 80's considerably helped glass to grow in popularity. Previously it was actually quite a tough product to sell. Jane says 'glass is now very much in fashion in this country and abroad'. The main problem now tends to be gaining the necessary experience to set up on your own.

"It is difficult finding work but you again have to research studios and keep contacting people. Look out for jobs being advertised in publications like Crafts Magazine. Talk to people and don't give up!"
Jane is a highly respected glass-blower, selling and exhibiting work both nationally and internationally. A hard craft to become established in, it has taken a great deal of perseverance to get to where she is today. However, she insists it is definitely worth the effort.

J.C.

Sales agents by Rosemary Jones

Rosemary Jones is one of very few sales agents covering the whole of Wales. As agents appear to be rather an elusive breed I am delighted that she has agreed to write a few notes on using an agent.

Have you ever thought about getting someone else to sell your products for you?

A sales agent could possibly help with that. I have worked as an agent for various companies for the last decade. The following observations are based on my own experiences and are intended as a general guide only. If you are interested in finding and employing a sales person it would be a good idea to get specialist advice. The laws in the UK and the EU deal with Commercial Agents .You can find out more on the internet too. People who are thinking about having an agent often ask the following questions:

1 *How does it all work?*

Briefly, an agent goes around an area with samples and gets orders. The orders are then sent on to the maker and the agent gets paid a commission for them.

2 *How much is commission?*

This varies between products and is negotiable. I work on commission of between 15% and 20% of the order value. I used to work for 12%. The commission is paid on the value of the order for the goods themselves; it does not include postage or VAT. Obviously it is not worth

Sales agents by Rosemary Jones

the agent's time if orders tend to be small, so a minimum order is useful.

3 *What's the difference between a minimum order and a carriage-free order?*

The minimum order is the rock bottom number of things a maker will send out before it is completely unprofitable. Carriage-free (or post-free) is the amount above which the maker will pay the postage. Usually that is what retailers go for as one less cost they will have to pass on to their own customers. As an example you could have a set of greetings cards with a minimum order of £50 and carriage-free £100, so the retailer would have to buy at least £50 but if they spent over £100 the maker would pay the postage.

4 *Is getting the orders all that an agent does?*

Good agents will do much more than just get orders; they can:

- give makers feedback about their products,
- give suggestions about new products,
- they can keep an eye on the competition and new trends in the market place,
- they can give makers feedback about particular customers,

all sorts of things - but essentially all they do is get orders. All the making, packing, invoicing, chasing money is done by the maker. Agents don't get paid if orders don't come in.

Sales agents by Rosemary Jones

5 *How do we agree on the area where the products are to be sold?*

This is negotiable but should be discussed carefully at the early stages. I work different areas for different people - and I do not cover the areas close to some makers because they like to do that themselves.

6 *Do we need a contract?*

Specialist advice would be good for this. I tend to have a chat with the people I am going to work for and once details are agreed these are either confirmed in writing or a more formal contract is signed, often with a clause saying that the contract will be reviewed within a specified length of time to make sure that both parties are happy with the way things are working.

7 *What does the maker have to do for the agent?*

- Provide samples and/or catalogues.
- Details of prices, quantities, postal costs.
- Payment arrangements, some people have discounts for prompt payers and interest charges for late ones.
- Order forms - useful but not essential, as long as there is somewhere for the customer to sign.
- Sending a commission statement of all orders that the maker owes the agent for. This is essential and should be done regularly (usually monthly). If the agent agrees with the statement, the agent sends an invoice and is paid. This is very important because it is also a record that orders have been

Sales agent by Rosemary Jones

received and not got lost somewhere en route.
- Pay your agent regularly.
- Pass on potential new customers details to agent
- Keep in touch

8 *How do I find an agent?*
- Word of mouth - ask successful makers how to find an agent
- Advertise at trade fairs and events by putting a notice on your stand 'Agents Wanted' or put an advert on notice board
- Internet research.

The good agents are often inundated with work so they can pick and choose, making it hard for a new maker to find someone willing to take them on.
If you start direct selling on your own, you may be able to learn from your buyers which are the sales agents that they like to work with, these would then be the agents for you to approach.

Agents often have a lot of other clients, so makers should not expect them to deal only with their products. When interviewing an agent it is usual practice to find out if the products in the agents' portfolio all complement each other - if you are a candle maker it is not very useful to have an agent who is already selling five lots of different candles. Find out how often the agent is "on the road" to see how busy they are and it is fine to ask who their main customers are. Agents can be a real benefit to a company and will help to boost sales.

Using a sales agent by Carrie Shapiro

Carrie Shapiro is a professional designer and business woman, she won the Welsh Young Business Achiever of the Year in 2004 and went on to represent Wales in the World competition. Here she shares her experiences in finding and working with an agent.

www.carrieelspeth.com

Carrie set up her jewellery business in 1999, starting off in a small studio in Cowbridge, Wales. She designed her jewellery using beads from the UK and abroad. She also designed a colourful range of cards and wrapping paper.

To find outlets she took samples and set off to discover suitable venues throughout the UK. This gave her invaluable knowledge of how the work was received and what the gallery/shop owners were looking for in her products. Carrie also attended trade shows; these are expensive to book and fees have to be paid up front, so Carrie was delighted to win an award from the Gift Association which subsidised space. She was also supported by The Princes' Trust. In this way she was able to afford to attend shows in the early days which helped to launch her work.

At this stage in her career The Princes' Trust had provided Carrie with a business mentor, she found his advice very helpful and was able to learn more about the benefits of agents. Around this time she was

Using a sales agent by Carrie Shapiro

approached by an agent who had seen her stationery at a shop and wanted to represent her. Luckily for her this arrangement worked well and although she went into it without too much research, and just a letter of agreement, it proved a satisfactory business relationship.

Now Carrie's business has grown she has moved into a 3500 sq ft building with a team of permanent staff; she also uses the skills of 20 self employed outworkers and she has 11 agents, each covering a particular region. This means that she must supply them all with a set of samples and keep them up to date with developments within her business. She does this through a monthly newsletter which highlights the best sellers, new designs and the sales of each agent etc.

Carrie has never gone to a solicitor to draw up a legal contract for her agents but has continued to use a more informal letter of agreement. As the agents are not her employees it is a delicate relationship to manage; she can instruct them to do things but cannot make them, and believes building a trusting loyal relationship is vital. She also sets realistic targets. Carrie feels that the impetus to earn a good living will inspire them to seek out sales for her, and follow up on previous outlets who have had orders and might need to be encouraged to order more. The agents earn a commission on all sales within their geographical area. If they are not reaching their target they are contacted to see why, as Carrie believes in keeping in touch on a regular basis.

Using a sales agent by Carrie Shapiro

Points to consider before taking on an agent:

- Gain experience and knowledge of what it is like to be an agent by trying to sell your own work to start with.
- Talk to other makers at shows, ask if they have agents and follow up recommendations.
- Ask the galleries and shops (when selling your work) if they deal with any agents, if so find out which they find good to work with.
- ✳ Don't put signs on your trade stand seeking agents, as you may be inundated with unsuitable applicants.
- Don't waste money on advertising; word of mouth is definitely the best method.
- Build a good relationship with your agent. To make sure they understand your work supply all the information you can. Spend time with them.
- Make it as easy as possible for agents to sell your work.

✳ Carrie believes that if an agent approaches you without you having to advertise it usually means they believe they can sell your product and will make a good effort of it. If the agent is not confident enough to approach you without a sign they are not going to be a very good sales person.

Carrie Shapiro www.carrieelspeth.com

Top: Sapphire Glass Rocks

Chunky Nuggets

Grants and Training

Boxing Hares by Willie Carter

Grants/Awards/Courses

As you will have noticed in the previous financial section most funders will require you to put up some money yourself. This can be a problem however if you are lucky enough to obtain a grant you may be able to use the grant money, as your contribution to the business loan. Unless, of course, the grant has been given for travel, research or some other specific area of development.

There are a variety of grant giving bodies to approach but again the first step should be to approach your local Arts Council of England office. (See page 27). Some, for instance, used to make a contribution to exhibition costs at the old Chelsea Craft Fair, if you were lucky enough to be selected. They will be able to tell you if they manage any suitable grants themselves, which you could apply for. If not they should be able to provide addresses of others who might be able to help.

Libraries and Career Centres usually stock directories like the 'The Directory of Grant Making Trusts' and 'The Grants Register'. The latter is intended for those at graduate level or above , who require further professional or advanced vocational training. It lists the financial assistance currently available from government agencies, international, national and private organisations; trawling through them is time consuming but could be worth while.

Of course the internet will also have most of the addresses but how to find them is the puzzle and you need plenty of time.

Grants/Awards/Courses

A number of funders are given below some have strict criteria for applicants, quite often geographical so if something is of particular interest to you please check carefully, nearly all provide details and forms to download on their websites.
www.artscouncil.org.uk
www.artquest.org.uk/funding

Laura Ashley Foundation
Mrs Annabel Thompson
3 Cromwell Place
London
SW7 2JE
For people looking for FE courses in textiles

British Council
Visual Arts Department
11 Portland Place
London
W1B 1EJ
T: 020 7389 3045
www.britishcouncil.org/arts/index.htm
Many useful sections on their site including funding and exhibiting abroad

Grants/Awards/Courses

The David Canter Memorial Fund
c/o The Devon Guild of Craftsman
Riverside Mill
Bovey Tracey
TQ13 QAF
T: 01626 832223
Each year a particular craft area is specified for awards,
ranging from £500-£1000. Applicants must have
completed their training and be working full or part-
time. The award is meant for special projects such as
setting up a workshop, buying materials/equipment or
for research and travel. Write for details with a SAE.

Ceramic Industry Forum
Federation House
Station Road
Stoke on Trent
ST4 2SA
T: 01782 415210
E:info@ceramicindustryforum.co.uk
www.ceramicindustryforum.co.uk/
New Talent Scholarships
Encouraging new, emerging talent is part of the CIF
'Leading by Design' initiative. Scholarships are seen as
vitally important by Universities to create effective links
between industry and design students.

Grants/Awards/Courses

The Winston Churchill Memorial Trust
15 Queen's Gate Terrace
London
SW7 5PR
T: 020 7584 9315
E: office@wcmt.org.uk
www.wcmt.org.uk
Applications are invited from any British Citizen with an individual travel project, which matches the categories listed by the Trust in that particular year. You will need to demonstrate that your project is feasible, worthwhile and will benefit this country on your return.
The list of categories and application forms are available from the end of June each year and must be returned by the third week in October.

The Clerkenwell Award
Workshop Manager
Clerkenwell Green Association
Pennybank Chambers
33- 35 St. Johns Square
London EC1M 4DS
T: 020 7251 0276
E: info@cga.org.uk
www.cga.org.uk
CGA wishes to help newly trained craftspeople set up in business within their own workshop. The Clerkenwell Award is to help subsidise the cost of a workshop during

the first 18 months of business and a package of business advice and support for the period. The Award applies to workshops located within the geographical area of Islington, Hackney, Camden and Tower Hamlets. Please note - the Award cannot be taken in conjunction with any other discounted workshop scheme.

Commonwealth Arts & Crafts Awards

Commonwealth Foundation
Marlborough House
Pall Mall
London SW1Y 5HY
T: 020 7930 3783
E: geninfo@commonwealth.int
www.commonwealthfoundation.com
A Biennial award open to craftspeople between 20 - 35 who are citizens of any Commonwealth country. The awards go towards helping the recipients explore their craft in another Commonwealth country - going towards travel, fees, living expenses and exhibition costs.

Crafts Council Development Award

44a Pentonville Road
London N1 9BY
T: 020 7806 2512
E: busdev@craftscouncil.org.uk
www.craftscouncil.org.uk

Grants/Awards/Courses

This award has no limits to the number of awards given or the disciplines which can apply. However anyone receiving other government 'start-up' awards cannot apply. A maintenance grant of £2,500 is divided into four payments of £625 over one year, it is intended to assist with costs of business and general subsistence.

An equipment grant can give up to £5,000, with the CC paying up to 50% of all eligible purchases. One to one support by a business development officer who will also pay two visits to assess workshop needs. Access to a creative mentor. A residential course in business training. Provision of 1,000 postcards, an opportunity to participate in trade fairs at home and abroad and inclusion in Photostore.

Next Move Scheme is a two year scheme, designed by the Craft's Council and North West Arts, to bridge the gap between education and your chosen career. It can provide funds of up to £7,000 towards maintenance and business development, if your are interested in setting up an independent business within a university department. Further details from: The Crafts Council

The Craft Potters Association
CPA Administrator
25 Foubert's Place
W1F 7QF
T: 020 7437 6781

Grants/Awards/Courses

The Craft Pottery Charitable Trust was established in 1991 and each year awards bursaries to enable students to carry out individual projects.There is an annual 'Setting Up' exhibition for new potters, names must be submitted by colleges, two from each will be selected.

  Each year, at Contemporary Ceramics in London, the CPA organises a Setting Out exhibition, which is designed to launch new graduates in their ceramics careers. Normally two bursaries are awarded each year.

The Goldsmiths' Company's Charities
Goldsmith's Hall
Foster Lane
EC2V 6BN
T: 020 7606 7010
Awards are made to students and apprentices in the precious metals and jewellery industry.
Getting Started is a **free** week-long course for recent UK graduates of precious metal courses. The aim of the course is not to dictate any particular career route for recent graduates: instead the aim is to provide an opportunity for attendees to review their options alongside a range of practical help and guidance .

The Harley Foundation Workshop Scheme
Welbeck
Worksop
Notts. S80 3LW

Grants/Awards/Courses

T: 01909 501700
E: info@harley-welbeck.co.uk
www.harleygallery.org.uk
They have custom-built workshop spaces for up to 30 makers. The workshops vary in size and are available to makers setting up for the first time under the 'seedbed license scheme' which phases in costs over a five year period. The Foundation makes one award, at the New Designers, of £1,000 plus one year's work shop space.

The Inches Carr Trust
Robin Blair
2 Greenhill Park
Edinburgh
EH10 4DW
T: 0131 447 4847
www.craftscotland.org
Annual craft bursaries of £4,000 are made to help the individuals develop their skills or a particular aspect of their work. For makers living and working in Scotland.

Oppenheim-John Downes Memorial Trust
c/o Whitefriars Street
London
EC4Y 8BH
Annual awards are made to deserving British makers, over 30 years of age, who are unable to effectively pursue their vocation by reason of their poverty.

Grants/Awards/Courses

The Princes Trust
Head Office
18, Park Square East
NW1 4LH
T: 0800 842842
www.princes-trust.org.uk
The Prince's Trust Business programme offers low
interest loans of up to £5,000 and support to enable 18-
30 year olds who are unemployed or under-employed to
start their own businesses. For people aged between 14-
25 The Prince's Trust can give from £50-£500 to help pay
for a course or the tools needed to take up a job offer.
To help with this they even offer a 'Test Marketing
Grant' which provides up to £250 to test the market,
where there is not enough proof to show the need for
your particular product already. They will offer one to
one advice and access to a variety of useful business
related information.The Trust also runs a shop in the
Kings Road, London which sells work produced by some
of the beneficiaries.

Queen Elizabeth Scholarship Trust
The Secretary
1, Buckingham Place
London
SW1E 6HR
T: 020 7828 2268
www.quest.org.uk

Grants/Awards/Courses

Awards worth between £2,000 and £15,000 for crafts-people of all ages living and working in the UK who wish to develop their skills. Scholarships are given to fund further study, training and practical experience in the UK and overseas. When selecting candidates for interview, the trustees look most favourably on those who have already demonstrated a talent and commitment to their trade or craft. Awards are not given for general further education courses or buying or leasing equipment and premises. Application deadlines second week in January & July.

Details can be downloaded or send SAE with 38p stamp

The Theo Moorman Trust for Weavers
Lisa Harms
14a Oakfield Road
Clifton
Bristol
BS8 2AW

As the title suggests this is only open to weavers living and working in the UK Applications are invited from weavers who have completed their training and have spent at least two years gaining work experience.

The awards are made every other year and can be for capital or revenue expenses, to enable weavers to enjoy a sabbatical, purchase equipment, pursue a project or develop their craft in any other way which the trustees think fit.

Grants/Awards/Courses

The Welsh Development Agency have a great deal of information on where to apply for grants and much more.
T: 0800 587 8101
www.wda.co.uk & **www**.financewales.co.uk

Wingate Scholarships
Administrator
20-22 Stukeley Street
WC2B 5LR
E:clark@wingate.org.uk
www.wingate.org.uk

Wingate scholarships are awarded to individuals of great potential or proven excellence who need financial support to undertake original, creative work. They are designed to help with the cost of a specific project which may last up to three years.

Not for any taught course or course leading to professional qualifications. Applicants must be citizens of the UK or other British Commonwealth countries, Ireland or Israel. Citizens of other European Union countries who are currently and have been for at least three years resident in the UK. Applicants must be living in the British Isles during the period of application (Feb-end March), and be 24 or over on September 1st of year of application.
Send A4 SAE with 41p stamp or download from internet.

Grants/Awards/Courses

The Woo Charitable Foundation

The Administrator
277 Green Lanes
London
N13 4XS
N.B Currently only accepting applications from those who have been established for ten years-so not relevant for new makers-unfortunately.

As you will have read in the previous pages there are several grants for those wishing to develop their skills or take time out for research. Although it is not easy to find funding for post graduate study, some Local Arts Councils may manage or know of small trusts or grants donated by local benefactors who have provided funding for particular specialist courses.

A number of the following groups, although helpful for general information, are not especially geared for art/craft related jobs or training - check carefully.

AGCAS

Association of Graduate Careers Advisory Services
c/o Careers Service
University of Sheffield
8-10 Favell Road
Sheffield S37 QX
T: 01142 753 381
www.agcas.org.uk

Training/Funding

Arts Council England
www.creativepeople.org.uk
The Arts Council says that this site 'offers you a wealth
of information on resources and events: workshops,
conferences, courses, mentoring schemes, critical
appraisal services and online tool-kits. You will also find
news about job opportunities and commissions. The arts
connect search enables you to look for such information
on the individual websites of our many partners.' If you
can't find what you're looking for, please contact them
and they will try to help.

Business Venture Capital Association
3 Clements Inn
London
WC2A 2AZ
T: 0207 025 2950
E: bvca@bvca.co.uk
www.bvca.co.uk

Career Development Loans (CDL)
www.lifelonglearning.co.uk
are available through a partnership arrangement
between four major banks. There are three elements to
a CDL; Course Fees, Other Course Costs and Living
Expenses. You can apply for your loan to cover one or
more of these elements and you can borrow anything
between £300 and £8,000. The loan can be used to

Training/Funding

cover up to 80% of your course fees plus up to 100 % of any related expenses. If you have been out of work for three months or longer at the time of application, you can apply for a CDL to cover 100 % of your course fees.

Crafts Study Centre (for research)
University College for the Creative Arts at Farnham
Falkner Road
Farnham
GU9 7DS
T: 01252
www.csc.ucreative.ac.uk

The Goldsmiths' Company Technology & Training
Goldsmith's Hall
Foster Lane
London EC2V 6BN
T: 020 7606 7010
www.thegoldsmiths.co.uk

Continuation of professional development is a key element of the work of the Goldsmiths' Company Technology & Training Department. A portfolio of specialist training has been created to support both graduates and those who are already established within the industry through a programme of masterclasses, seminars and other professional development activities.

Training/Funding

The Learning Skills Council based in Coventry has over 40 regional offices offering advice on further education.
T: 0845 585 505
www.lifelonglearning.co.uk

The National Council for Graduate Entrepreneurship NCGE
3 Priestley Wharf
Holt Street
Birmingham
B7 4BN
T: 0121 380 3545 E: contact us@ncge.org.uk
www.ncge.org.uk
(NCGE) will raise the profile of entrepreneurship and increase the number of students and graduates seriously considering and engaging in business start-up in all its forms including self-employment. The NCGE connects students and graduates and stakeholders.

National Glass Centre
Liberty Way
Sunderland
SR6 0GL
T: 0191 515 5555
E: info@nationalglasscentre.com
www.nationalglasscentre.com
Cultural centre dedicated to the exploration, creation and promotion of glass.

Training/Funding

NESTA
Fishmongers' Chambers
110 Upper Thames Street
EC4R 3TW
T: 020 7645 9538
www.nesta.org.uk
Creative Pioneer Programme
NESTA's Creative Pioneer Programme offers business skills training, but in a new way. It's a unique opportunity for individuals at the early stages of their careers (up to five years post graduation) to access knowledge, training, support and business funding. The application deadline is early September for the next year

London Printworks Trust
Unit 7, Brighton House
9 Brighton Terrace
SW9 8DJ
T: 020 7738 7841
E: info@londonprintworks.com
www.londonprintworks.com
The UK's leading textile print resource which offers a diverse range of activities, professional development advice and a project management service.Including a membership scheme, printmaking facilities,courses, workshops, advice, exhibitions and 'Creative Connection' for 16-25 unemployed people living in Lambeth.

Training/Funding

Creative Connections call their hotline:
T: 020 7738 5774 or
E: creativeconnection@mail.com

Shell LiveWIRE
Design Works Unit 15
William Street
Felling
Gateshead
Tyne & Wear
NE10 0JP
T: 0845 757 3252
E: shell-livewire@pne.org
www.shell-livewire.org
Helps 16 -30 year olds start and develop their own business and hosts a national 'business start-up' competition

Small Firms Loan Guarantee Scheme
Level 2
St. Mary's House
c/o Moorfoot
Sheffield
S1 1PQ
T: 0114 259 7308/9
E: SFLGS@sbs.gsi.gov.uk

Proposal

Once you have identified a grant/award for which you would like to apply you will need to prepare your application proposal. The previous sections, on assembling your self promotion kit and portfolio will, I hope, have helped draw your attention to some of the points to remember.

Each funder will have drawn up their own specific criteria. It is therefore essential to study these **before** filling in the forms. Criteria will often require some or all of the the following to be covered:

- Evidence of commitment to continue as a **professional** in your chosen practice.

- evidence that you have achieved a high standard in your work,

- evidence to show your creative potential,

- explanation of how the grant will help with production of new work,

- evidence that you have: researched your market, taken professional advice in preparing your business plan and that your plan is realistic,

- A portfolio of your work and or original pieces.

Presentation

The next step may be to make a presentation to the actual funders, employers, client or commissioners. Some people are quite comfortable selling themselves 'face to face', but many others find this very difficult. Several of the cases studies in this book mention situations where they had to face interviewers, for one reason or another. Once you have your own business up and running you will often be in the situation of selling yourself to your clients.

Forward planning is once again the most important

- Try to find out before hand exactly what is expected of you,

- How long the interview will be and with whom,

- Should you take samples of your work- if so how many,

- Check the criteria for the particular grant/job etc.

- Research as much as you can about the company/people in question.

- Check that you know how to ge to the venue and plan the journey to allow plenty of time.

- If you require equipment for the presentation check that everything is ready and working.

Presentation

- Consider any awkward questions which might arise and think through some good answers,

- Check through the article on negotiation p140.

Armed with so much information you should feel far more confident. As Matthew Burt p148. said try to be enthusiastic about your product/design as this will be passed on to the your audience, but try not get carried away. When the time comes for the actual presentation try be as professional as possible in your approach; listen to the questions and consider before you speak i.e don't start talking too much. You know your work well and you are the best person to sell it, so just relax and enjoy the opportunity to talk about yourself-it doesn't happen too often!

 If you are lucky enough to obtain a grant, you will probably also benefit from the back up system set up by the trust or body who have made the award. If not you will find the following useful"

Your local **Business Link Office** is ideal for this service, as they provide a one-stop-shop for business information and support services. They do not aim to provide off the shelf packages but rather work with their clients to build up long-term relationships with the Businesses which they help.

Somerset runs 'Small Business Start-Up' where they offer a one to one session with a specialist Counsellor, to

Business Support

discuss your ideas and point you in the right direction. This will be followed by the opportunity to join a three day course giving practical, hands on, guidance on the wide range of business issues you may meet. Many other offices may offer similar courses but all will include most of the following services :

- Business information and advice.

- Business reviews and planning.

- Overseas Trade Services.

- Innovation technology and design counsellor.

- Business skills seminars.

- Managing people.

- Training & development.

- Issues & business regulations.

- Marketing advice.

- Financial packages advice.

- Business start-up and counselling.

Business Support

Your local Chamber of Commerce can be another useful resource to join. **www**.britishchambers.org.uk
An active Chamber of Commerce can provide:

- Business opportunities, contacts and support

- Representation (lobbying)

- Networking

- Help with Exporting

- Access to information and advice.

Working on your own, you can feel rather isolated. Membership of your local Chamber of Commerce, Craft Guild or Society can help. As a member of a particular group, as discussed earlier, you will receive newsletters and make contacts who you will be able to call on when you need advice-networking.

The National Federation of Self-Employed and Small Businesses
Whittle Way
Blackpool Business Park
Blackpool
FY4 2FE
T: 01253 336 000
www.fsb.org.uk

Business Support

A non-profit making & non political Federation which protects the rights of the small business. For a nominal annual membership fee services include: telephone advice lines, payment of legal and accountancy costs to deal with tax, VAT, health & safety, motoring prosecutions, employment and pay disputes. A bi-monthly magazine and a free regional magazine listing your local office and events.

The Enterprise Centre for the Creative Arts
London College of Printing
The London Institute
Elephant & Castle
SE1 6SB
T: 020 7514 7985
E: info@creatingaliving.org
www.creatingaliving.org
Offers free one-to-one advice on setting up or running your own business, plus online information on from financial, legal and funding experts. there are over 400 online support network and business directory links.

www.exchangelondon.org
A group of specialist London Universities have amalgamated to create an online business development support system.

Business Support

Design Factory (East Midlands)
Units 7/8 Navigation Wharf
Carre Street
Sleaford
NG34 7TW
T: 01529 414532
E: hayley@designfactory.org.uk
www.designfactory.org.uk

Creative Capital
3 Wilkes Street
London E1 6QF
T: 020 7375 2973
E: info@creative-capital.org.uk
www.creative-capital.org.uk
A network of arts organisations providing advice,
information and professional development opportunities
for artists and art professionals across London.
*Although this site is apparently supported by the Arts
Council it is a confusing site to use and repeats much of
the information provided more clearly elsewhere.*

www.arts.ac.uk/student
University site general inf

Willie Carter Case study

Willie is now a well established potter, who benefited from a Crafts Council Setting Up Grant a number of years ago. Here he describes how he got started and his attitude to running a business.

It might sound obvious but if there are any grants available, whether from the Crafts Council or local authorities, do apply for them, there is nothing to lose. If you are successful in getting a grant then well done, if you are turned down it doesn't mean that your work is bad.

One probable reason is that there isn't enough money to go round, so basically grant or no grant get on with setting up your business.

- Find somewhere with cheap rent,

- Try and avoid borrowing money, you don't need the latest equipment,

- Make do without it and adapt or buy second hand.

Willie Carter Case study

I first read about the Crafts Councils' 'Setting Up' grant in Crafts Magazine. It was the final year at college so I took slides of work, made for my final exhibition and applied. When the letter of rejection came, it didn't make any difference to my plans to set up in business. I was determined to do this whatever happened.

Three months later I applied again-with the same set of slides! This time I was invited down for an interview in front of a selection panel. Thankfully this was not the formal procedure I had expected. There were six people seated round a large table, including Janice Tchelenco who was representing the pottery side of things.

Willie Carter Case study

The atmosphere was relaxed and informal and questions were related mainly to college life and work and any influences from existing potters. One particular area in which they were interested was what would happen if the grant wasn't forthcoming. At that point the workshop premises were already secured so I was going to continue regardless of the outcome. I am convinced that this resolve to carry on with my plans strengthened my application, as it showed my commitment towards starting the business.

The grant was structured in two ways. There was a payment for equipment, on the understanding that I put up the other half. This enabled me to buy an electric kiln and wheel, which I am still using! The maintenance part was then paid in installments which was used for basic running costs. Knowing that regular money would arrive throughout the first year was very reassuring.

All this was in the early '80's, not a particularly good time for new businesses. The recession was just kicking in and selling pots was difficult. Thankfully things have steadily improved, over the years, and the business is still going 20 years later **but it has to be worked at constantly.** I'm not sure that people setting up today will

Willie showed perseverance in trying for a Setting Up Grant twice (Kathleen Hills also had two interviews); so don't be too disappointed if not successful first time.

Willie Carter Case study

have an easier time than I did but there are certain things to consider which might help. **One of the fundamental things to consider is :**

- that of establishing good relations with your potential buyers. I am still supplying galleries who I contacted 19 years ago !

It is not a good idea to turn up at a gallery hoping to interest them in buying your work-something I found out the hard way!

- Do some research beforehand and identify places in which your work might fit in. Initially, contact by phone, then go to the gallery with your work. You're wasting your time turning up with slides or photographs, seeing work "in the flesh" is best.

- Once your work has been accepted keep in touch. Gallery owners are busy people and with the best of intentions don't have the time to contact makers, even if they have sold all the work.

- Good quality trade fairs can be a useful way to show your work. They are expensive to do but are an excellent way to make new contacts.

- One word of warning, make sure that you are in a position to fulfil large orders, don't take on anything no matter how lucrative sounding which you can't produce.Originally from Michigan (USA),

Willie Carter Case study

- Join your local crafts associations which usually organise several exhibitions a year. They also provide the opportunity to meet other crafts-people in your field who can provide a wealth for ideas and experience.

- Above all be confident in your work and don't be put off if it seems that at first you are constantly being turned down. You might be in the craft business for the next 40 years so don't expect everything to happen in the first couple of years.

W.C.

Pam Campanelli Case study

Pamela Campanelli established herself as a jewellery maker in 2000, she works from her home-studio in Essex. Her mother, who used to make things with beads when Pamela was a child, first introduced her to this craft. Although her higher education was not art-based, her passion for jewellery remained. She learned the  silver-casting technique at the age of 17 and enrolled on several evening classes while studying at university. Later Pamela worked as a full-time research statistician - which was her chosen career. It was in this line of work that Pamela transferred to the UK in 1991.

In 1997 she decided to change her career path and focus on something more creative. Between 1997-2000 Pamela experimented with various artistic disciplines and attended workshops run by George Grant. She had a few commissions, mainly from friends, and took part in a few exhibitions. She also continued to work part-time in research to provide financial support, to buy most of the equipment she needed.

In January 2000 she was ready to set up as a serious jewellery-maker, using her garden shed as a studio.

Shortly before this, Pamela had ordered a copy of Second Steps. She says that she found the guide extremely helpful and constantly referred to it for advice in the early stages of her jewellery making career.

Pam Campanelli Case study

Of particular use was the importance the book placed on making a one year business plan; which was especially useful because it helped her to set realistic, achievable goals. As Pamela points out, the first year in business is definitely one of trial and error, therefore having some type of guideline is essential. She also found the **information provided on approaching galleries**, promoting work and useful organisations to be of great value.

Inevitably Pamela had a couple of bad experiences in her first year, (which on reflection) she happily describes as disastrous. The first was a craft fair in Colchester, which she thought would be precisely that. Instead she found herself sitting amongst people selling homemade crafts more suited to that of a village fete. So her hand-crafted jewellery was not particularly high in demand! Another time Pamela exhibited with two watercolour artists which was fine, except all the visitors wondered why jewellery was being displayed, at an 'art' exhibition. They did not realise it was actually for sale. It is therefore important to be selective in your choice of show, and do research. Pamela joined the Craft Movement (no longer trading), in 2000 and through this organisation began to meet and exhibit with like-minded makers. More significantly the visitors were serious buyers thus making the chances of selling work more likely. As Pamela said, establishing a clientele is of great importance. In November of that year she exhibited at a

Pam Campanelli Case study

show specifically for jewellerymakers and sold her first serious amount of work.

Since 2001, Pamela has steadily built up a good client-base through galleries, the internet, private sales and commissions. She keeps her clientele well informed about her latest work and exhibitions via regular mail shots. Pamela has decided to keep her business small scale and still works as a part-time research statistician; not so much for financial support but rather because it allows her to travel and provides a change of scenery. As she points out, although her garden shed studio has now been transferred to a plush conservatory, working from home can sometimes be a strain.

P.C.

Index

Cushions page 320
by Neil Bottle